A Believer-in-Waiting's
First Encounters with God

elizabeth mahlou

MSI Press

For information, contact:
MSI Press
1760-F Airline Hwy, 203
Hollister, CA 95023

Library of Congress Control Number 2010943485

ISBN 978-1-933455-28-0

cover design by CDL Services

Printed in the United States of America

Table of Contents

To the Reader

My first intent was to call this book *Hierophany and Contemplation* because that is how my life with God has unfolded. However, the more time I have spent writing this book, the clearer it has become that a simpler title would serve better. That is when I remembered the appellation given to me by friends in Jordan a few years ago: believer in waiting. They refused to accept my professions of atheism and chose instead to view me as a lost lamb whom God would scoop up sooner or later, which, indeed, God did.

Along with scooping me up, God gave me the task of writing. Although I did not understand what that task was to encompass, I did know that this writing was not to be more of the professional books I publish but rather writing for the glory of God and especially for those who might also be lost lambs, believers in waiting, souls chased by the Hound of Heaven, or whatever other label one might use. It is a task that I sometimes find overwhelming and that I, admittedly, don't always want to do. It is, in fact, with some reluctance that I pen this book for I am certain there are readers who will consider my tales tall and my experiences outlandish. They sometimes seem that way to me, too.

Yet, I must assume that if these kinds of things happen to me, then they probably also happen to other people, who may be even more reluctant than I to share them. I understand their reluctance. After all, William James called the great Catholic mystics psychopaths. What equally unpleasant labels might be applied to us lesser souls who today experience supernatural phenomena? Equally disturbing is the tendency of some fundamentalists to attribute all mysticism to evil spirits, which baffles me: if they consider demons capable of communicating with us directly, why would God not be able to do the same? Do they really consider God less powerful than Satan? "It is a terrible evil," says St. Teresa of Avila (*Interior Mansons*), "to doubt that God has power to work in a way far beyond our understanding."

Although often unbelievable to those who yearn for something that fits human reasoning, our relationship with God is a simple matter if we let God direct it. I forget that all too often. I want to learn from the great theologians of the centuries. I forget that the greatest Teacher of all is standing by to help. Sometimes I wonder if my yearning for greater clarity, for more input, for better understanding annoys the Great Teacher. There are indeed times when, as I read some renowned treatise about God, I feel as if a Hand is attempting to cover the page, to pull me back from the mode of reading to the mode of listening. I am reminded at these times of de-Caussade's caution in *Abandonment to Divine Providence* that we should rely upon God and not upon the interpretation of others. As one continues to walk with God, one sees previous experiences in a new light while the brilliance of one's first encounters with God remains as a ubiquitous star, illuminating where one has been, is now, and will be going. That reality lies at the core of the experiences shared here.

On a housekeeping note, I confess that in the first chapter of this book I have repeated my conversion story and a couple of other passages from my book, *Blest Atheist*. I have included only those few that are critical for understanding my post-conversion experiences.

On another housekeeping note, I should mention that Elizabeth Mahlou is the pseudonym I used in writing *Blest Atheist*. The frank sharing of the details of an explosively violent childhood could potentially have done more harm than good. So, to avoid harming those who have harmed me, I chose to remain anonymous. An equally important reason for using a pseudonym is the nature of this volume. This book is not about me. It is a love song to the Divine, and without a person to publicize as the author, I hope the focus will stay where it belongs: on God. I have used my own life as the content only because what do we really know except that which we have personally experienced or witnessed? To maintain anonymity, I have had to alter some names and locations. Events are true. It is the naming and locating of them that sometimes has morphed along with details that might be too revealing.

I would like to acknowledge a special group of people: readers of the prepublication manuscript. Many thanks to Marie Cosgrove, Renee Espinola, Peggy Guillory, Dr. Geri Henderson, Anne Laforge, Anais Mora, Barbara Muck, Dr. Rebecca Oxford, Anne Marie Peloquin, Debb Rodriguez, Silvia Sanchez, Alice Sousa, and Julie Trudell for reading the draft of this book. Their comments have improved the book; any errors or omissions that remain are mine.

Finally, I should say that had everything been up to me, I would have kept the contents of this work to myself. Many of the events that have occurred in my post-conversion life are personal. As such, they are the kind of thing that should remain between God and me. However, I have felt such a push to put them on paper that I assume (hopefully, accurately) the Divine has a need for someone to know of them.

Upon rare occasion, I find someone who shares some of my experiences. For both of us, the finding of each other becomes mutual comfort. Perhaps there is someone out there in the wider universe for whom this book is meant to be such a comfort, and if that is the case, the writing of it will have been worth the effort.

Then, too, there are the Bible verses that keep falling under my hand. For example, we are told in *Matthew* 5: 14-16 not to hide our light but rather to be witnesses for God: "You are the light of the world . . . let your light shine before others that they may see your good deeds and glorify your Father in Heaven." Keeping hidden the gifts that God has given me and the assigned tasks that God has facilitated seems out of accord with this verse. And so I write of them and place this book in your hands, dear readers, to do with as you will.

elizabeth mahlou

A Simple Grace

It all began with prayer, but which prayer began it all I do not know. It may have been the grace I was coerced into saying just five years ago. Or, it may have been the prayer of my sister Danielle five decades earlier. I used to think it was the former. Now, in reviewing the whole expanse of my life, I rather think it may have been the latter.

Danielle's Prayer

The "8-pack," a moniker given to my seven younger siblings and me by my brother Rollie, suffered immense abuse during our childhood. My sister Katrina, in fact, never planned on growing up, certain that she would be killed by Ma before reaching adulthood. However amazing, we all did survive the extensive physical abuse (e.g., being stabbed, thrown into walls, kicked into unconsciousness, pulled down flights of stairs by the hair, and much more), emotional abuse (e.g., being negatively compared with each other, denigrated at every opportunity, and, in one instance, forced to sit on the stairs for hours, expecting to be deliberately set on fire at any moment), and sexual abuse (various male relatives had their way with both the boys and the girls). We had each other for support: the 8-pack was very important to all of us in an age when neighbors and teachers looked the other way. Remarkably, contrary to what most of today's psychologists would expect, we reached adulthood without any lasting evidence of physical abuse or any significant emotional scars.

After coming to faith, I commented to God, "If only You had been with me during those earlier, difficult days, how much easier it would have been." To that, a quiet, impressive Voice that always startles me when I hear it, responded "I *was* with you." Had I only known!

That interchange reminds me of the experience of St. Anthony, the third-century desert father. As described in *The Life of Anthony of Egypt* by St. Athanasius, St. Anthony once hid in a cave to escape demons. The demons reached him anyway and seemed to have beaten him to death. His servant brought him out from the cave, and the other hermits prepared to mourn his passing when he unexpectedly revived and demanded that his servant return him to the cave. There he called out to the demons, who returned to attack him. This time, they were stopped by a bright light which Anthony knew to be the presence of God.

"Where were You before," asked St. Anthony, "when the demons were beating me so badly?"

"I was here," God replied. "I wanted to wait and see how well you fought for yourself."

Telling this to Danielle as we walked about the moon-flooded Maine woods one night while visiting my brother Keith, I remarked that I found it unfathomable as to why we would be so protected by God. One can find any number of stories about children who did not survive abuse. Why should *we* receive special treatment? She looked at me curiously and said, "I thought you knew."

"Knew what?" I asked.

"What all the rest of the 8-pack knew."

"What??"

"The first thing I remember in my entire life—I think I was only two or three years old—was realizing what a predicament we were in, and I said a prayer: 'Dear God, Dad is gone all the time, and Ma is a child. So, would You please raise us?'"

It took more than fifty years for me to learn about that prayer. Upon reflection, I believe that neither my siblings nor I were ever far from God's sight, protection, intentions for our lives, or even the tendency to use us to help others. That could only have been the case if God had answered the prayer of a precocious toddler.

Why would I think that God answered that prayer? Because I am alive today, having survived a dangerously abusive childhood. Because my children are alive today in spite of two having been born with multiple birth defects so severe that doctors gave them little hope for survival, let alone the generally cheerful lives they now lead. Because I have been chronically happy all my life when a person not protected by God might have attempted suicide. Because I am incurably optimistic even though I endured years of poverty and seven clinical deaths of my children. Because I can see where my siblings and I have been used for helping people in ways that we could not have accomplished alone.

And maybe mostly because I don't know where the parachute has always come from when I have been in the process of falling off a cliff if it has not been being held out to me by God. I have always taken the parachute. I never used to say thank you because I did not think that there was Anyone to thank. At the same time, I never questioned that there would be a parachute if I needed it. It would appear that I had a tacit relationship with God on a subconscious level while totally oblivious to any sense of God in the conscious world—until the day of the grace.

My Prayer

The evening began like most of my after-work evenings with my colleague, Jean, and me grabbing a bite at whatever local eatery happened to be open at the late hour we finished the next piece of the project were working on. The project fortunately fell into the period of time after I had returned from the Middle East and before my husband, Donnie, who stayed in Jordan for another six months to finish his contract, also returned. Living alone, I had ample time for extensive work commitments. So did Jean, who also was living apart from her family at the time. Thus, we found ourselves in a string of restaurants, relaxing, at least once a week.

While our conversations were typically light, I quickly learned that Jean had some deeply held spiritual beliefs. Not one to belittle such beliefs—after all, I had just spent two years in a part of the world where everyone prays five times a day— but also not sharing them, I would sit quietly while Jean said grace before our meals. Quietly, that is, until one night when Jean astonished me.

"It is your turn to say grace tonight," she announced.

"You've got to be kidding!" I stared at her in total disbelief.

"No," she responded. "I mean it. It is your turn to say grace."

"You don't ask an atheist to say grace!" I retorted, nonplussed. Why was she doing this? She had respected my atheism until now.

"I did ask," she said softly but firmly. "And I'm not going to eat until you do."

Well, this could be a long, hungry evening, I thought. I shook my head in amazement at her self-assurance. What was going on in that head of hers?

Jean was an immigrant from the Middle East. Perhaps that facilitated our friendship. I was comfortable with dark features, Middle Eastern customs, and the open and giving, yet corrective and expectant nature of Middle Easterners. Other than her national origin, there was little special about Jean on the surface. She was taller than I, but then nearly everyone is taller than I. She would certainly not have been labeled tall by anyone else. She had a quiet way of moving and an easy acceptance of American customs. We talked about work mostly, about our families some, and about the Middle East a little. We never discussed religion, God, or my atheism. It was an implicit understanding that we accepted each other's beliefs for what they were without trying to convince one another of anything different. Now, however, Jean's soft, insistent voice was urging me to pray.

"Look," I answered. "I simply cannot. Just go ahead and eat. Please."

"No," Jean shook her head. "I am not going to eat without grace being said, and it is your turn. Just try!"

"You say it," I insisted.

Again she shook her head. "It is your turn." So this was the outcome of my graciously having agreed to let her say grace at earlier meals!

"I don't want to!" The pugilism that propelled me undeterred through my abusive childhood took over. Perturbation turned into anger.

"We all have to do things we don't want to." She just was not going to give up!

"I don't know how!"

"Well, just say whatever comes into your head."

She seemed quite serious about not eating until I said something. I, though, had no idea what to say and no desire to say anything at all.

We sat in front of a small, square, wooden table with a red-and-white checkered tablecloth pulled across it diagonally and time seeming to stand still. Nearly alone in this non-descript pizza kitchen with non-descript, about-to-be shared, and quickly-growing-cold pizza pies sitting on the table between us, we simply stared at each other. Who would win this battle of stares? I waited for her to give in, to say grace herself, or just start eating, but that did not happen. I could not understand what had come over her, why she was behaving this way.

Later, I learned that her unpremeditated words had surprised even her. She had planned to say grace, as she had before, yet other words came out. Having said them, she felt an overwhelming need to stand by them, a need that she could neither explain nor ignore.

So, I was the one to give in. What harm could a few meaningless words do? At least, we would get to the dinner that was quickly growing cold.

Grace? I searched in my mind for the right words. I searched for *any* words. I tried to remember some of the words Jean had used, but I had not really listened.

Blessing. I remembered that. You have to say something about blessing, I figured.

"If You truly exist, bless this food, and bless us with Your presence," I muttered with annoyed audacity.

Bless us with Your presence. Vacuous words. Or so I thought. They rolled off the tip of my tongue meaninglessly. Good, that was over. At least, now we could eat.

I picked up a piece of pizza. We must have been hungry when we ordered. Two medium pizzas steamed in front of us: a vegetarian pizza and a deluxe combination of meats and vegetables. That was a lot of food, but after a long day and evening of work, I was quite ready to ingest a sizable portion of the meal in front of us.

Then it happened. Presence we had! Strong Presence. We both felt it. It was as if we were encompassed by a diaphanous entity, gentle in love and firm in persistence. I was immediately and completely disoriented. Not only were we surrounded by Presence, but also something had entered inside me, down to the cellular level, filling me with an expanding internal Presence that connected with the external Presence. Fr. Thomas Dubay in *The Fire Within* describes infused prayer as a divine invasion, but this Presence, thrust upon me without warning, without any expectation that any Divine Power really existed, through a door that was not intentionally opened, was no mere invasion; it was a divine occupation. The Gospel of Mark tells us that we have to give permission to God to heal us, help us, and be with us. I suppose that my words had done just that even if my intent was nothing of the sort.

I breathed with difficulty. I thought only randomly. I don't remember our conversation that evening, so consumed was I by this Presence. Nor does Jean. I do not remember if I ate. I do remember the restaurant closing seemingly too early and a strongly perceived need to continue talking. Jean felt that, too. We walked around the peninsula, looking for a place to sit. We talked as aimlessly as we walked. Jean seemed not to want to leave the Presence, and I wanted not to be left alone with It.

Jean and I stopped beside the ocean, sat on the beach, and talked for perhaps an hour. Incomplete sentences. Incomplete thoughts. Still caught in the diaphanous Presence. The evening was coming to a close, and we both needed to return home in order to catch some sleep before going to work the next day. Were it not for that, we might have spent the entire night on the sand.

Since then, I have often wondered why God would self-reveal to an unholy person rather than exclusively to holy ones. While I have learned that humans trying to make sense of the Divine is an absurd undertaking, I did find a possible explanation recently when I read Richard Rohr's book, *Things Hidden*. "Strangely enough," writes Fr. Richard, "it's often imperfect people and people in quite secular settings who encounter the Presence." Fr. Richard goes on to state that this pattern is clear throughout the Bible. He further points out that the most unlikely and sinful people have been used to do God's bidding, as I was to find out in the months and years following the evening in that nondescript restaurant. The *Bible* tells of these, too: Samson the seduced, Saul the killer of Christians, and a host of others we could all name.

So, let's see: imperfect, sinner, secular, unbeliever... I am starting to understand. I was a pretty good candidate for God to show up and say, "Whoa, there! Here I am! Follow Me!"

Ultimately incapable of saying "no" to God, I now find myself scrambling over difficult terrain along a very narrow path, trying to keep up with those giant-sized footsteps I agreed to follow instead of independently choosing my road through life. Although I no longer determine my own direction, the journey is more meaningful and pleasurable. I especially like the part about not being alone: "Behold, I am with you always, even to the end of time" (*Matthew* 28:20).

But I get ahead of myself. On that evening in 2006, I was not yet ready for the "being with always" part. I was confused even by the "being with now" encounter.

Two Weeks

I felt disoriented driving home. I was still disoriented the next morning and remained disoriented for the next two weeks. The Presence simply would not leave me. I felt like I was caught in a cosmic nutcracker. "I won't crack," I swore to myself and said the same thing to Jean. "I am like a Brazil nut. My shell is strong and hard."

The strong shell, materialized from my natural tendency toward defiance, had hardened during years of protecting myself from abusive adults as a child and from abusive health-care providers and other so-called "helpers" as an adult, those who were supposed to help me improve the life of my "exceptional" children but often, in well-intentioned ignorance, did the opposite. All my life I had fought: abusive adult relatives, sexual predators, muggers, bureaucracy, schools, doctors, you name it. I had built an impermeable shell around any vulnerability. I stood ready to fight the Presence, to fight any idea that contradicted my atheistic conviction that the universe existed ungoverned.

That seemed not to matter. The Presence kept gently squeezing the Brazil nut in the cosmic nutcracker ever tighter, ever so gently, ever so persistently. Minute by minute, hour by hour, day by day, never varying.

The more the cosmic nutcracker squeezed me, the more I thrashed about in its pincers, fighting back. Like Francis Thompson, I "fled" the "hound of heaven" "down the nights and down the days" of the next two weeks. I thought I had already escaped God in "the arches of the years" and in the "labyrinthine ways of my own mind." I was comfortable in my atheism. To now find a divine "hound" at my heels, doggedly pulling at my coattails, slinking into the recesses of my consciousness, and woofing into the warp of my sleep, unnerved me.

When I found that I could not flee the "hound" at my coattails, I turned, like a trapped animal, and fought. That is, after all, what I knew how to do best. I fought, as usual, not from fear but from anger. I attempted to repel this Presence, and when I was unable to do so, I confronted and blamed It.

Never before had I questioned why I bore children with birth defects. Not considering that there might be a God to intervene, I accepted that Donnie and I did not have a felicitous combination of genes and therefore two of our four children suffered from multiple defects. My question, when confronted first with my younger daughter Noelle's birth defects (spina bifida, hydrocephalus, and epilepsy) and then with my younger son Doah's 18 physical birth defects and mental retardation, was not "Why?" but "What do we need to do to keep them healthy and prepare them to lead worthwhile lives?"

Only now, with this Presence occupying my thinking space day and night, did the errant thought come to me, "Why?" If a deity existed, then I could accept these birth defects and other tribulations I had experienced with equanimity only if that deity were effete, but nothing seemed effete about this Power that had me in its grasp. Bewildered and hostile, I wanted answers, and I demanded an explanation.

The Book of Job

Read the *Book of Job*! The words slammed into my consciousness in a manner I found four years later described in Jeremiah: "Is not my word like fire, says the Lord, like a hammer shattering rocks?" (*Jer* 23:29). I accepted these quiet but compelling words at face value and then surprised myself by following them instinctively, without examination, so strong was the Presence in and around me.

While the response to my question came immediately, the answer took days to understand. I knew that *Job* was in the *Bible*. So, I found a *Bible* on line.

On first reading, the meaning of *Job* escaped me. Well, there is the expression, the "patience of Job," but I did not think that the message I was supposed to be getting had anything to do with patience. After all, how does lack of patience explain why children might be born with handicaps?

So, I read the *Book of Job* again. I read about all the torments and testing, about how Job remained faithful through all the tests. I did not think that was the message I was supposed to be getting, either. That, too, did not explain why my children would be born with handicaps. My children are not torments. They are delights.

So, I read the *Book of Job* a third time, paying attention to how Job's friends exhorted him to turn his back on God, but instead he turned his back on their advice. This, too, did not seem to be the message I was supposed to be getting for I had neither blamed God nor believed in God at the time of my children's births. It seemed I would need the patience of Job to ferret out the meaning.

So, I read the *Book of Job* a fourth time and began to feel much empathy for him, especially in the loss of his children. I noted well that I had been spared such pain even in the case of Doah, whose first two years took the form of a dance between life and death and life again. An understanding was beginning to emerge but not one that I could yet articulate.

I read the *Book of Job* a fifth time, and then I finally got it. It was not the concept of patience that I needed to understand, nor was it a test whose requirements I needed to meet. No, it was the concept of *agape* (the unconditional love described by C. S. Lewis in his book, *Four Loves*) that I needed to develop. No matter what was taken from Job or what he had to endure, he continued to love God. What the message of *Job* said to me at that time is that God's presence in our lives and what happens to us and those we care about are separate things. God has promised to be with us if we allow it. What happens to us, on the other hand, is often a result of free will with which God does not usually interfere. My children's birth defects, in a parallel way, were an unfortunate combination of genes, resulting from the free will of two people who chose each other as marital partners. Even with the animal kingdom, God allows genetics free play. God could have chosen to intervene but did not do so. There likely are reasons for every bad thing that befalls us where God does not intervene, and there likely are reasons for my children's birth defects. Certainly, my being unaware of the reasons does not mean that they do not exist. Just as likely, were I aware of them, I might not understand them. Scripture tells us that God's thinking is as far above ours as the sky is from the earth. The reasons, in any case, are irrelevant. Our love of God must be as unconditional as is God's love for us. What happens in life—the bad things and the good things—cannot be conditions for whether or not we love God. They are tangential.

The reading of *Job* began to answer my question as to why God could exist and not intervene or why it might even be better to allow the birth defects to occur, as counterintuitive as the latter may sound. My children's value is not defined by their birth defects but by what they do with their lives, how they help others, what they contribute to the world, i.e., not by what they *cannot* do but rather but what they *can* do and *do* do.

There was one more thing. God protected Job. It did not seem that way to Job because Job was not in on the agreement that God had made with Satan. Satan could take things away from Job and then, later, God even allowed Satan to torment Job physically. Job, however, was never in danger of dying. His life was always in God's hands as so many times have been my life and the lives of my children when I, like Job, could not see what was transpiring.

As I came to know God better, I began to understand the story of Job in new ways. One important thing I now understand that would have made no sense in the beginning of my walk with God is that God does not owe us anything. God does not owe us a life without trouble. God does not owe us peace and tranquility. God does not owe us intervention at any particular point in our lives or at all. God sometimes assuages our pain because God wants to. That assuaging is an act of grace, not an entitlement.

C. S. Lewis (The Problem of Pain) points out that we would not ever expect pain to be assuaged were we not to believe in a loving God. It is the concept of a loving God that creates the "problem of pain" because we assume that a loving God would not want us ever to feel any pain. I now understand, however, that any assumption that it is God's will that our lives be free of hassle, pain, and even death is a wrong assumption. When we assume that a loving God would want to heal us of all our illnesses, prevent the loss of our relatives at too early an age, or destroy all our enemies, we fail to understand that every intervention, every assistance, every gift (including the gift of suffering) is a grace. Our God-given compassion for our fellow man tells us that human intervention is good. Perhaps that is our basis for expecting God's intervention, but we are not privy to the kinds of knowledge that God has. Nor are we capable of seeing and understanding the human condition in the way that God does. We are told in the New Testament that the way of the cross is both necessary and good, and St. Pio specifically points to this way as essential to our spiritual development: "In order to grow, we need hard bread: the cross, humiliation, trials, and denials." Yet, it is the way of the cross that we attempt to avoid when we demand to know why bad things happen to good people. Might it not be arrogant to believe that any one of us should be exempt from the pain and suffering that comprises the human condition? As St. Paul told the Ephesians, "we are all by nature deserving of wrath" (Ephesians 2:3). Some may experience little pain, thanks to God's mercy. Others may experience much pain, also thanks to God's mercy. I did not come to understand this continuum of mercy until I had passed through a series of metanoias.

Simply by asking the question why God would allow us to experience pain, we separate ourselves from God—another understanding that took a long time to settle in among my logic-driven neurons. Bonaventure suggests that God does not observe our suffering from afar but rather suffers with us from within, that out of an abundance of love God is drawn to those who suffer. I now fully believe the words of God to me: "I *was* with You" during your childhood. In one of my favorite books, *The Humility of God*, Ilia Delio beautifully provides a touching description of this co-suffering:

> *Suffering is . . . the place of transformation. It is a door by which God can enter in and love us where we are. . . As Clare of Assisi realized, God bends down in the cross to share our tears out of a heart full of mercy and love . . .*
>
> *The power of God is the powerlessness of God's unconditional love shown to us in the cross. God is the beggar who will not force his way into our homes unless we open the door. . . . God shares in the brokenness of the world out of the abundance of divine love.*

Suffering, then, should be welcomed. "Tribulation is a gift God gives us," St. Thomas More tells us, "one that he especially gives his special friends." St. Rose of Lima concurs, "Without the burden of afflictions, it is impossible to reach the height of grace. The gift of grace increases as the struggle increases."

Was my question answered? Not completely. I still did not know for certain why God intervened to save my children's lives but not to prevent their birth defects. However, I have come to understand that knowing is not important; trusting without knowing is paramount. Knowing can be detrimental to a relationship with God. One could take the Israelites as an archetype in this respect. When God let them know things more fully, they turned away from God. Likewise, when Adam and Eve began to know, they strayed. So, I accept not knowing as an inherent condition for real trust, a strong relationship, and deep conversion.

In his homily recently, a visiting priest told the story of three people who went to learn from a guru. The guru asked them why they had come to him. One replied that he had heard of the guru through local people and wanted to learn from such an august man. The guru sent him away. The second replied that she had looked around to see who could teach her what she wanted to learn and in this way had discovered the existence of the guru. He sent her away. The third stammered out that he really did not know how he had heard about the guru or what he really wanted to learn. The guru replied, "You'll do."

Clearly, to the guru, not knowing was desirable. Maybe, if I continue to accept the not-knowing part of my relationship with God, I, too, will one day hear the words, "You'll do."

I like to think that perhaps this is what happened in the case of my children. Perhaps God looked for parents who would love them just the way they are and fight for them to be everything they could be without knowing the reason for their physical and mental challenges and said of Donnie and me, "these parents will do." I like to think that even though I was an atheist and Donnie an agnostic, God thought that we just might do.

God entrusted some very special people to us: children with wide smiles, great love for people, and needs that have allowed people with whom they have come into contact to help them in ways that have been mutually rewarding. Because of their ability to bring smiles to others, I call our children God's rainbow makers. Just like a broken sprinkler gushes more water onto a parched field, creating rainbows all around, God's rainbow makers sprinkle more water onto parched souls, creating rainbows within. The thought that God blessed and entrusted me with these rainbow makers entered my head only after a very long pondering on the experience of Job. Realizing the extent of God's trust in me has engendered within me a reciprocal trust in God.

Two Requests

By the time I had finished reading *Job* for the fifth time, two weeks of living in the Presence had passed. Two weeks had taken their toll on my endurance in unsuccessfully fighting to free myself from a diaphanous Presence, felt and heard but unseen. So, I came to a full stop. I had found myself in what T. S. Eliot in "Four Quartets" called "the still point of the turning world."

The constant pressure from the cosmic nutcracker was opening this Brazil nut. There seemed to be nothing I could do to prevent that. So, in the spirit of the best defense being a strong offense, while driving to work on morning, I took a small leap of faith—small, because, after all, with the Presence with me all the time, it did not take much faith to admit it existed. So, I dared to make two requests, testing the waters of my growing conviction that this Presence might, indeed, be God.

On the Surface: Requesting Help from God

For nearly three months I had been trying to help Janie, the wife of one our employees, find a job. She and her children had been living two hours away for a year, and this was taking a toll on the family. She had applied to our division but did not have the right background to be hired by my organization although we kept her application on file just in case. I had networked with colleagues in appropriate fields in the local community. All were sympathetic. None had jobs to offer. It seemed hopeless. So, I ventured a prayer, this time a real one, albeit one that expressed as much doubt as hope: "I give up. I cannot help Janie. If You really exist, please help her."

While I was at it, I thought, I might as well make a second request. One of my colleagues had used up nearly all her sick leave because of a recurrent illness that she seemed unable to conquer. This had been going on for nearly six months. So I added a couple of lines to my please-find-Janie-a-job prayer, "And, if you will heal my colleague, Janet, I will go to church." I have no idea what prompted me to make that promise. It came out of the blue.

After making the requests, I remember feeling that my life was about to change in uncontrollable ways. Somehow I *expected* those requests to be granted. Answered requests, though, would mean only one thing: God exists.

When I arrived at work, I opened my email as I do at the beginning of each work day. As usual, there were more than 200 notes to read. Most of them were information about deadlines, requests for meetings, or general announcements. One, however, was different. It came from a director of another division. "One of my managers, Robert Shaw," he wrote, "served as an external member of a hiring committee for your division recently and noticed the resume of Jane Lane. Robert tells me that Jane's background does not fit any of your positions but precisely fits our need for a position in our production shop that we are just about to announce. Would you release her application to us?"

I was stunned. I read the note again. There was no doubt any more in my mind of God's existence. The answer to my very first prayer of petition had come in less than 30 minutes. Like St. Thomas, the doubting disciple, I did not want to believe. Like St. Thomas, I had to believe: "My Lord and my God!"

Now I was nervous about the request I had made for Janet. One should not bargain with God, I thought. So, I amended my request and promise, "Never mind. I will go to church without any conditions and trust You to heal my colleague."

Two days and one interview later, Janie had accepted a job offer. I had arrived at the end of a lfe-changing two-week period. I knew that since Janie had found work, Janet, my sick colleague, would get well (she did). So, now I had a promise to keep.

Under the Surface: Trusting God

There was more going on unconsciously in the making of these two requests than I recognized from the surface phenomena. First, there was that *expectation* for answered prayer. Where had that come from? There was also that willingness to trust God *without* prayer first being answered. That was even more surprising. Where had *that* come from?

I now make little concrete connection between answered prayer and willingness to believe, a connection that Darin Hufford in *The Misunderstood God* claims is a common mistake: "We focus on the things we want from God, and if we get them, we trust Him. If we don't, we won't." For me, the connection to God has little to do with getting wants satisfied. The seedlings of trust grew out of that very first expectation that God would help someone in need. Today, my tree of trust is not rooted in God answering my prayers in the way that I would like but rather in knowing that God, even without my asking, will take care of others and me in ways we need. Over time, unconditional trust has come to be a cornerstone of my relationship with God.

Presence in the Past

Following the appearance of the Presence, I spent much time in retrospection. Such activity was unusual for me since I am by nature impulsive, not reflective. It was, however, necessary. I was still chewing on those words, "I *was* with you."

In retrospect, I realized that something about God was very familiar. There has been a pattern in my life of getting what I need, not necessarily what I want but something better, even when I do not know in advance that I need it. Did that have anything to do with Danielle's prayer? Was this the result of God parenting us?

If so, how ironic! I never believed that there was a God. Yet, I also never felt alone. That is truly hard to explain. I anthropomorphized the universe itself, and that is how I dealt with the no God but not alone phenomenon.

To a great extent, I never really thought much, as an abused child, about the meaning of the universe. I was more concerned with staying alive, convinced that I *would* survive but also thinking that I had to do my part to make that happen. The thoughts of a child are neither coherent nor rational, so it is hard to unravel them.

Having encountered God in my present made recognizing God in my past easier, finally seeing the tenuous connections and the moments of protection. Nearly everywhere I found God's fingerprint. I guess this is what many people used to feel when they met me, why they were confused by my profession of atheism, and why they considered me a believer in waiting. In my intense atheism, I had ignored repeated evidence of miracles, angels, and God-surround times. I don't know whether there has been more of the miraculous in my life than in the lives of others or whether most people, like myself of the past, overlook the miraculous either because they cannot believe it (too good to be real), will not believe it (does not fit with their concept of how the universe works), or do not anticipate it.

Tenuous Connections

In *Blest Atheist*, I related in detail the remarkable medical rescue of Shura, a dying child artist from Siberia, and a host of miracles associated with him. When I wrote that story, I was unaware of the greatest miracle of all, one that predated everything that happened. That miracle, the story of a weeping icon, became known to me only a year after my book was published.

In Siberia during the Cold War

Shura was born with spina bifida, a debilitating and sometimes fatal birth defect, in Akademgorodok, Siberia, a place in the wooded-steppe outskirts of Novosibirsk where I had done research, consulting, and teaching, and my second most favorite place in the world, the first being the little mission town I live in right now. I was attracted to Siberia from the beginning of my Russian studies in the 1970s, finally making it there with my older daughter Lizzie in 1984-1985 for the purpose of studying Siberian dialects of Russian. In Siberia, there is an expression, "the mink whistles at me," meaning that one is attracted to something for some compelling reason, does not know why, and cannot resist. When it came to Siberia, the mink whistled at me.

The winter of 1984-1985 was cold in more ways than just the deep snow across which 11-year-old Lizzie, our Siberian friends, and I cross-country skied, one of the few leisure activities in the wooded steppe when all is frozen over. The Cold War between the US and USSR was still in its below-zero stages, so it was somewhat of a surprise that the mink's whistle was strong enough to force the hand of the Foreign Student Office at the University of Moscow to allow Lizzie and me to go to Siberia. No one had gone there to do research in Soviet times. (My trip there with Lizzie opened the door to later scholars.)

One of the most instrumental people in getting the university to change its mind was Dr. Alexandr Ilich Fedorov, the head of the Institute of Philology at the Siberian Branch of the USSR Academy of Sciences in Akademgorodok, where I did my research. Aleksandr Ilich, whose dictionaries were key to my research (*"oni mne kak zoloto*," I told him, meaning that they were like gold to me—this pleased him mightily), became my consultant, friend, guide, and Siberian father. Years later, he was quite pleased when he learned that I had befriended Shura, who was beloved in Akademgorodok. He felt that through me he had contributed to Shura's great story and miracle, and, of course, he had.

Back to Siberia after Raspad

Ten years passed between my research days in Siberia and my first contact with Shura. In 1993, I was sent to Krasnoyarsk, a Siberian city on the Yenisei River, by the Soros Foundation, which was assisting the new Russian government in establishing an educational system supportive of democratic reforms in the wake of the dissolution of the Soviet Union (*raspad*). A delegation from Novosibirsk came to Krasnoyarsk to study with me. The delegation was headed by Mila Beresova, a nondescript 40-something with long hair, a strong will, and a high level of competence in whatever she undertook. When I learned that Mila came from Akademgorodok itself, I asked her if she happened to know Aleksandr Ilich.

"Of course," she answered. "He was my *nauchnyj rukovoditil'* (graduate student advisor) when I was in graduate school at Novosibirsk State University."

I was happy to hear that Mila knew Aleksandr Ilich because I had a favor to ask her. "Would you tell him that I received the letter he sent to me last month?" I asked. "I did not get a chance to answer it before leaving to come here because my daughter, Noelle, was in the hospital. However, I will answer it upon return, and I can help him with his request for publication assistance."

"Certainly, I will tell him," she responded and asked, "Why was your daughter in the hospital?"

"Nothing dramatic," I said. "She has spina bifida and so ends up in the hospital periodically for one thing or another."

"Spina bifida?" Now Mila was genuinely interested. "My godson, Shura, has spina bifida. He is frequently in the hospital. The doctors there are now telling us that his days are numbered because of infections and gangrene in his legs for which we have no antibiotics."

Then and there plans were made to try to bring Shura to the United States for care. Tenuous connections indeed! Had it not been for the joint connection of Mila and me with Aleksandr Ilich, the topic of spina bifida would not have come up. Had that topic not come up, I would never have learned about Shura.

About Shura

Shura, a remarkably talented teenager, had twice had his art work exhibited at Dom uchenykh (House of Scientists, which recognizes the leading academicians and artists in Russia), his poetry published in a collective volume, his art and verse for children published as a monograph, and a television documentary made on his life. Shura was unusual in other ways, too. Born with spina bifida during the Soviet era in a region with a paucity of antibiotics and no experience with these kinds of neurologic defects, accompanied by extremely harsh winters with temperatures dipping lower than 75 degrees below zero, it was remarkable that he had survived. Moreover, he was born into a family of seven children (nearly unheard of in the USSR—housing the family required two apartments) and grew up homeschooled in a country where such a thing was not only unheard of but also rejected out of hand.

Shura's form of spina bifida, lipomyelomeningeocele, is moderately debilitating. He ambulated with crutches and, occasionally, on his knees. Over time, as a result of untreated ulcerations typical in enervated skin, he developed gangrene in both legs.

Shura's family kept him alive against all odds. When there was no longer any hope of keeping him alive in Siberia, they handed him over to a stranger (me), fully trusting God to watch over him. They never questioned why God had sent them an atheist from the West, and I never questioned that I was supposed to help Shura.

Shura's mother, Mara, was the faith center of the family. A small woman with short, dark hair, propelled by endurance beyond all imagination, she worked as a teacher during the day, including homeschooling her handicapped son, and a family activities coordinator (necessary with seven children) at night. She knew that Shura was God's special child, and she made sure that Shura knew that: he came to me full of faith even if I had none.

Shura's father, Lev, walked with an energetic limp. As a child in Belarus, he was wounded during WWII when a bomb fell and did not detonate. Curious children in the town examined the bomb, which rolled away and exploded. A piece of scrap metal struck Lev in the leg. As with his son, Shura, Lev's leg injuries kept him from physically demanding activities and gave him time for intellectual and artistic pursuits. He was a dreamer and printing press owner.

Told of the plan Mila and I had formulated to get Shura to the United States for medical treatment, Lev and Mara tirelessly gathered money from worldwide visitors to Akademgorodok to make this happen. When Lev delivered Shura to me, he handed me a large bag of coins and bills from many different countries, not enough to pay for anything of a medical nature but enough to help with clothing and feeding Shura, which was significant assistance, considering that Donnie and I were eking out a living from two self-employed careers that barely fed the six children already living with us, our four and two others we had taken in.

Getting Shura to the United States

Gettting Shura to the United States depended upon more tenuous connections. What had occurred previously in my life had not only put me into contact with the people I needed to effect Shura's life-saving medical care but also prepared me to help Shura emotionally and physiologically. After all, who better to provide assistance to a spina bifida teenager from Siberia than a mother of a spina bifida teenager from America? Who better to pry a visa out of the U. S. Embassy in Moscow than a former State Department supervisor who had trained many of the diplomats working at the embassy? Who better to provide a home to a speaker of Russian than someone who spoke Russian? Who better to help a child of the cold Siberian winter assimilate into California sunshine than a grown child of the cold Maine winters now living in California? Who better to help a child from the wooded steppe than an American researcher who had lived and worked in the same steppe, loved the steppe and its people, and knew its literature and its culture? It would seem that all my experiences and knowledge worked together for a purpose. Not only was the preparation for this purpose amazingly complete, but any one missing component would have made it impossible to help Shura. That is why I describe Shura's life as a flight on the wings of serendipity.

Strapped for Cash

Once Shura reached the United States, the swooping, rising, and falling of that flight followed a path that led to more miracles than one might ever imagine in the life of one person. The first few weeks, though, seemed like a free fall. While doctors were ready to donate care, no hospital would donate a bed. Hospitals required $50,000 up front, preferably in cash, and advised us that the full cost of care would easily reach $500,000. We had not foreseen this obstacle.

Shura settled into our household routine in California while we pondered the next steps. He was a gangly lad. It was hard to tell how tall he was since he could not stand or walk. However, not being able to walk did not hold him back. He never sat still. He scooted all over the house, searching out activities, food, and playmates. Twice a day, he bathed his legs in betadine to kill as much as possible of the gangrene that was trying to kill him.

We began looking for help in the traditional way: we contacted the media. Newspapers and television stations carried his story, but help was not forthcoming. A videographer made a captivating children's video, using Shura's artwork, and Orthodox churches in California and Washington, D.C. sold copies.

The Orthodox Church connection was also a matter of serendipity. Rick Berman, our connection to the Orthodox churches in California, had coincidentally made the acquaintance of Shura's family while on a trip through Siberia. In Washington, Nadezhda Long, a former colleague from my State Department days, helped us. Her grandfather had authored a famous book about St. Petersburg, a book with which Lev was familiar. Nadezhda's deceased father had been a Russian artist, and her educated and compassionate mother, Tatyana, knew Russian art inside out. The connection to Nadezhda and her mother turned out to be a comforting one for Shura, preparing him to undergo surgery in a foreign land with greater ease, having spent some time with people who understood him and his art. The number of coincidences was piling up. Only a die-hard atheist like I could have failed to see the hand of God behind them.

John Kluge, Metromedia

With the sales of Shura's books and videotapes, more dollars tumbled in, but we were desperately far from the amount of cash we needed with time passing far too quickly. Yet, as luck would have it (or not have it, as it seemed at the time), I had to stop the desperate search for funding long enough to attend a conference in San Diego. Lizzie, who was then an undergraduate student at the University of California at San Diego, offered to help sell copies of Shura's video and book at the conference.

On the last day of the conference, a marvelous thing happened. A graduate student at Virginia State College, Cindy Reginald, stopped to look at Shura's book and hear his story. "Have you thought of contacting John Kluge?" she asked.

"Who is John Kluge?" I responded. The graduate student explained that he was the third wealthiest American at that time. He was the founder of an international communications company, Metromedia, which had branches in Russia. She promised to send me his address.

Sure enough, just a few days later, she did. I wrote a plaintive note to Mr. Kluge, asking for any amount of help that he could give. To show the talent (and thereby the "worth" of Shura), I included a copy of his art book and the videotape.

At the same time, Shura and Lev learned about the Orthodox Church in San Francisco. They felt that a trip to that church and a talk with the priest there would help. I drove them there. We met with the priest, who accepted a heaping helping of books and videotapes to sell. While at the church, Shura and Lev stood at the icon of St. John the Wonderworker and asked St. John to intercede on Shura's behalf.

On the way back from San Francisco, we stopped at the post office, and I mailed my package to John Kluge. It was worth a try! I had some hope because I was an inveterate optimist. Shura and Lev had some hope because they had their faith.

Four days later, that hope reached fruition in the form of a phone call. The voice at the other end was pleasant and emanated a sense of competence and care.

"This is Nurse J," the voice said. "I am the coordinator of the spina bifida clinic at Virginia State Hospital. We have been contacted by John Kluge, who would like to sponsor Shura Ivanovich. I have in my hand two tickets if you will come here, and the hospital has already received a check from Mr. Kluge for $500,000."

Would we! Off we went to Virginia, just in time. Shura's gangrene had so damaged his legs by the time we reached Virginia that both had to be amputated.

Shura was bedded for his surgeries at the Kluge Rehabilitation Center at Virginia State Hospital. This center, it turned out, had been established some years earlier through the generosity of John Kluge. I had unknowingly contacted a philanthropist with a long-standing interest in the very medical area that plagued Shura and with an ex-wife who patronized art.

And herein lay a series of miracles, the first of which was how the letter got to Mr. Kluge in the first place. When I mailed him a thank you note, the letter was returned to us as "no such address." Indeed, we had been given erroneous information. First, there was no such zip code. Second, John Kluge had not lived in Virginia for years. He lived in New York City. Nonetheless, within 96 hours of mailing the package from California, it had reached New York City (via Virginia) and a check for a half-million dollars had reached the hospital. I don't understand how that happened, but it did. I was grateful to Lady Luck. Lev and Shura were grateful to God and to St. John the Wonderworker.

The Moleibin and the INS

God wasn't finished yet, though. Shura had asked for a *moleibin* (prayer service) prior to his surgery. Nadezhda Long arranged for it to take place during a Tuesday evening feast day celebratory Mass at St. John's Orthodox Church in Washington, D.C. Due to the last-minute arrangements, the *moleibin* had not been announced. Nonetheless, the service was well attended.

After the service, as is the tradition in Russian Orthodox Churches, everyone shared a potluck meal. Many people spoke to Shura and me about his situation, but one man in particular stood out. He kept looking our way, then finally stood up, came over, and held out his hand.

"Hi, I'm Max," he introduced himself simply with his first name. "I'm curious. Did you have any trouble getting a visa for Shura?"

Hearing that question, I let loose with our litany of troubles, the year-long effort it had taken to pry a visa out of the American Embassy in Moscow. Max listened politely, then informed us that his job was to oversee the INS and also the consular officers at embassies.

"I'm not surprised that you had difficulties," he concluded, handing me a card. "The system is set up to prevent abuse, but sometimes it weeds out legitimate cases. I know who you are now. Here is my home phone number. Call me if you have any problems in the future."

On the way home from the *moleibin*, I told Nadezhda about the meeting with Max. She had talked to him, too.

"I was surprised to see him there," she told us, "because he moved to Baltimore a year ago and goes to church there now. He told me he was working late tonight and felt compelled to observe the holy day of obligation with us on the way home."

How handy for us that Max stopped at the service on the one night that Shura was there for we would need his help. We called Max several months later when we ran into problems with a California INS office that did not want to extend Shura's visa. Max took care of the problem in less than a day.

Gurney-Side

Once Shura was back at the hospital, another wonderful coincidence stepped into our lives in the person of Dr. Vasilii Kirillov. Vasya (the Russian nickname for Vasilii) was a heart surgeon, visiting from the Ukraine. He heard about a young boy from Siberia, who did not speak English and would be undergoing a double amputation, and he appeared at the door to his room. I met Vasya right before the surgery. Permanently etched into my memory is the view of him walking beside Shura's gurney to the room where Shura would be anesthetized. As a parent or guardian, I could not follow Shura into the pre-op room or into the operating room, but Vasya could go with him every step of the way—and did. Throughout Shura's recovery and subsequent life in the United States, Vasya spent time with him, discussing Russian literature, the motherland, and those things that only Russian men talk about among themselves.

From Then to Now

Shura's post-surgery care would take months. After a couple of trips from California to Virginia for follow-up care, Nurse J, who had at one time been an art teacher, made an offer. It was one that none of us could refuse but also one that would again change lives.

"Why not let Shura move in with me?" she asked. "My son, Jason, is his same age, and I know how to care for spina bifida needs. Besides, I have spent twenty years as a nurse, working with parents of spina bifida children, but I have never parented one myself. This would be a good experience for me." I was not sure that she knew all she was volunteering for, but I accepted. Shura's family back in Siberia concurred.

Today Shura says that he is luckiest boy in the world because he has three mothers. Nurse J, Mara, and I became great friends. Today Nurse J and I are as much like sisters as any blood sisters could be. After all, we have been American-mothering the same child for a long time.

Shura stayed in the USA for 15 years. He returned to Russia in January 2009 to be with his aging parents, a return made possible because antibiotics are now readily available in Russia. We had, we thought, approached the end of a story of miracles and tenuous connections that brought together many people who would not have otherwise known each other and who felt blessed by their involvement in what appeared to be a divine plan.

An Epilogue

Just when we thought we had completed the puzzle, the picture expanded. A few months after Shura returned to Russia, Nadezhda Long called me from Washington. She had been reading a newly published book and wanted to share a story from it with me.

"Beth, you are simply not going to believe this," she bubbled over the phone. I wondered what could be so exciting.

"Remember Max?" she asked.

Remember Max? Without Max, Shura would have long ago been shipped back to Russia, before his health had stabilized. Without Max, Shura might even be dead now. And, of course, who could not forget the oddity that Shura's unannounced *moleibin* was the only Mass at St. John's that Max had attended in the year since he had moved to Baltimore and, in fact, was the last Mass he ever attended at St. John's. I mentioned all this to Nadezhda, commenting that his appearance that evening seemed nothing short of miraculous.

She cut me off. "Oh, we did not know but a small part of the significance of Max being there that night!" she exclaimed. Now she had my attention!

"Max is a convert to Orthodoxy from atheism, and his story is included in this book about a special icon." Instantly, I liked Max even more. His story paralleled mine—but it did not. What Nadezhda then related to me left me speechless.

"Years ago," she said, "an icon that wept oil with healing powers was brought from Europe to the United States, where it was presented at a number of Orthodox congregations. Among these congregations was our church, St. John's, and among the congregation was a blind boy, who had lost his eyesight to disease. When doctors could not help, his parents brought him to the icon in an attempt to try anything to help their child. When the icon passed by the boy, it began to weep oil. The priest placed the oil from the icon on the boy's eyes, and the boy saw. From that day on, he was no longer blind. And from that day on, his parents, Max and his wife, having converted from atheism to Orthodoxy on the spot, have been devout worshippers."

Had there been no icon miracle ten years before Shura was born, there could have been no miraculous appearance of Max on the night of Shura's *moleibin*. How extraordinary are the ways of the Lord!

Protected

Many times in my past I have felt protected. For a long time, it was an anthromorphized universe that I assumed would protect me. Later, I realized that all those years God had been watching over my family and me—and is still doing so.

Safe in San Ignatio

San Ignatio is surrounded by hills, gentle slopes that rise enough into the sky to be considered small mountains but not great summits. As such, they exude an atmosphere of friendliness, like the hand of God reaching out to say, "Here I am; come nearer." I see these hills every day. In the winter and spring, when they have been sprinkled with raindrops, they are great folds of green carpets spreading toward the sun. When the rain has sunk below the roots of the grass, they become the golden hills of our summer and fall. Whether they are green or gold, I can look upon them and know that my help comes from just beyond them, from God, who pours out love with the sunshine and with the rain. When I take my daily walk, I often find myself reciting *Psalm 121*, as I look upon the hills. Here, indeed, I find my help. Here, too, I find that God never sleeps. The sun by day and the moon by night in our clear sky remind me of God's presence, love, and kindness. Here I feel secure.

One dark night at the parish in San Ignatio, I was the last to leave a meeting. As I exited the door, the visiting priest who had led the meeting stood in the doorway. Surprised, I asked him what he was doing.

"I am watching you until you reach your car."

"I hope you have great long-distance vision," I replied, "because I walked here from home." Home was several blocks away, an easy and safe walk.

"In that case, be careful," he cautioned me, "I wouldn't want you to be attacked."

What a strange thing for him to say, I thought. Aloud, I said, "I am not worried. I feel protected."

In a quiet voice that seemed to come from a sudden understanding, he responded, "I believe you are." I believe I am, too.

Puerto Rico

Not only do I feel protected, but also I have no explanation for why I am here today other than having been protected in the past. Whether it is dreamily walking in front of cars—growing up on a Maine farm without much in the way of roads probably contributes to that habit—or being placed in harm's way due to my occupation, I seem to escape injury regularly.

In 1980, my reserve unit had been called to active duty in Puerto Rico to replace sailors who had been attacked, wounded, and killed on the way home from the night shift at a military post. My unit, considered one of the most ready in the reserves at that time, was activated to fill in the decimated ranks until those wounded returned to duty and those killed replaced. I left my graduate studies and university teaching position and took off for exotically dangerous work on an island. There I found myself the officer in charge of mid watch (the night shift).

The four armed US Marine Corps guards in the bed of a pickup truck in front of our bus on our way to work and another four in a pickup that followed it reminded us of the seriousness of our situation, as did the single Marine, with rifle locked and loaded, crouching beside the bus driver. I sat in the front seat, behind the Marine and right a young, wide-eyed military policeman whose greatest task in civilian life had been mall patrol.

For days, we had no incidents and were becoming blasé about our exotic assignment until the return to our lodging from our final shift before leaving the island. As the early morning sun began to reveal the surrounding fields, we were wending down the dirt road leading from the military post to a major highway when a herd of cows unexpectedly separated us from our front Marine guard. As the last cow crossed the road, a white panel truck deftly inserted itself in front of us. The Marine on the bus looked at the driver, Rudy, a reckless, tough guy from our home unit, and said, "This is what happened the last time. The next thing that will happen is that people inside the truck will open the back doors and begin firing. When that happens, duck, and let me return fire."

"They are going to open those doors and shoot us?" Rudy asked incredulously. "The hell they are!" He stepped on the gas and rammed the bus into the back of the panel truck. Matching his speed with that of the panel truck driver, he literally pushed the panel truck all the way to the highway, where the truck then passed us by. A couple of would-be killers inside pointed rifles out a side window at us, but they did not dare start a public fracas. Off they went, and home we went, having been protected by Rudy, who, I suspect, had been given divine inspiration and courage.

Little Doah and the Big Highway

One Sunday morning Doah, our younger son, in the simple follow-through-on-desire-without-regard-to-consequences manner that characterizes mental retardation, decided to take a walk down the middle of Lee Highway in Arlington, Virginia. That is a dangerous place for adults and animals, even for cars, let alone a seriously retarded four-year-old who was supposed to have been waiting for me on the stoop while I grabbed my purse and car keys.

Realizing what had to have happened when I saw the empty stoop, I began walking down the highway, looking into the side streets, calling his name. At the third intersection, a man appeared from the side street and asked, "Are you looking for a little blond boy?"

Relieved, I confirmed that I was. "Have you seen him?"

"Oh, yes," he said. "We have him at the church on the next block. We found him wandering down the highway and took him into the church to figure out who he was, but all he could tell us was that his name is Doah, his father's name is Daddy, his mother's name is Mommy, and he lives at home."

"Yeah," I sighed. "We have not been able to teach him standard responses."

That we found Doah is amazing. That Doah survived a four-block walk down a six-lane highway is even more remarkable. Protected? I think that Doah even today is frequently protected because he cannot protect himself.

Angel on the Highway

While a student at the University of California in San Diego, Lizzie was returning home late one night from a babysitting job. Route 5 was a mess—mounds of construction. She slowed to the posted 45 mph speed limit. Suddenly, behind her, a drunk driver, flying through the curves and barricades at a speed later estimated to be 90 mph, rammed her from behind, thrusting the truck she was driving into one of the concrete walls. The truck rolled away to the center of the road, stopping with the passenger window on the ground and the driver's window facing the sky. Lizzie did not have the strength to open the window, so she turned and tried to egress through the small cab window above the truck bed.

"Hold on a minute! Stay put, and I will help you!" The voice of a burly construction worker called across the road from the construction site.

The man, wearing a plaid shirt and work jeans, quickly reached Lizzie's side. He kicked in the driver's window and pulled her through. Then he carried her to the construction site and waited with her for the ambulance, which he, being the only worker at the site, had called. He helped her onto the ambulance and said good-bye, soothing her with the words that she was going to be okay.

At the hospital, the doctors examined her and decided to keep her overnight even though she seemed uninjured. They praised her for wearing her seat belt and told her how remarkable it was that she had no injuries at all.

Lizzie had just drifted off to sleep when the police showed up. They took her report of the accident but stopped her when she described the construction worker.

"No, that makes no sense," the police officer told her. "A passing truck driver called in the accident to 911, and the ambulance drivers said that they found you wandering around the construction, dazed and alone."

Well, here was news! As soon as Lizzie was released from the hospital, she viewed the truck at the place to which it had been towed. The window *was* smashed, but she had no scratches at all. How could she have kicked out a window that was above her head, let alone without getting any scratches? No, clearly, she had had help.

Her next step was to call Caltrans, the California state department responsible for the construction site to find out who had been working at the site the night of the accident. The answer: no one. However, Caltrans did survey its workers and ran the story in its news media to see if some Good Samaritan had been there that night. The response: all accounted for during that time frame, no one at the site. Perhaps a plaid shirt and work jeans are the garb *du jour* for a contemporary angel.

Metanoia

With the awareness that the Presence that had enveloped me was indeed divine, I knew my life would change in spite of my initial resistance. (There is some comfort in knowing that I am not alone. In *Deep Conversion, Deep Prayer*, Fr. Thomas Dubay speaks of the "remarkable resistance that most people place before significant moral change happening in their lives.")

What I did not know was how deep the change would become, that this transformation (*metanoia*) would continue without end, and that I would, at times, stall it. St. Bernard of Clairvaux is reputed to have said that "there are more people who are converted from mortal sin to grace than there are religious converted from good to better." I have indeed occasionally placed obstacles in the path of a potentially transformative experience, the first of which was opening the church door.

The Church Door

Entering the church the first time was difficult. The question of where to go never came up. When I made the promise to go to church, the image of Old Mission Church, part of the mission located just two blocks down the street from my house, popped into my head unbidden. I had no idea what denomination Old Mission was, but whatever it was, it would become mine.

The weekend after I made my promise to God, I walked up to the doors of Old Mission for Saturday vespers. The doors were closed, and people were singing. I was two minutes late. I walked over to a bench in the garden outside the church and sat down. I knew I should go in, but I had no idea what I would find inside. If I was not yet ready to enter the church confidently as a new believer, I was certainly not ready to enter it late.

Near me in the garden was a family: mother, father, and three children. Tourists, I thought. They were taking pictures of the roses. Suddenly, they grouped together, looked directly at me, and then headed toward the church as if they had been sent to show me that it is permitted to walk in late. They opened the door and entered. June, as I have later learned the mother's name to be, held the door for me until, after a moment's hesitation, I followed her through.

The family boldly marched down the middle aisle of the 3-aisle church. I stood tentatively at the door, searching for an inconspicuous seat. Noticing that I was standing beside an unoccupied pew against the back wall of the church, I slunk into it and sat cautiously upright. Next to the door—an easy escape if needed, I thought! The words of the person reading something at the distant front of the church barely made their way to my ears. With the murmur of these half-heard words in my head, I looked around the church uneasily. I felt like an interloper at best, an imposter at worst. What was I doing here? I recognized no faces, but I did recognize my feelings.

It was as if I had suddenly found myself in a foreign country with no cultural preparation and no understanding of the language.

No one noticed either me or my uneasiness. They were all intent on reciting, singing, standing, sitting, kneeling in an order that made no particular sense to me. I did understand the most important thing: the church was Catholic. "God, what are you thinking?" I wondered. "You want me at a Catholic church?"

Catholic liturgy was alien to me. Thanks to my experience with Shura, however, I could follow the service where there were similarities between Orthodox practices and Catholic ones although, ironically, I had no idea what words were used in English. I had been exposed to the liturgy only in Russian. Never had I been to any Catholic celebrations or ceremonies. Had I misunderstood where God wanted me to be? Did the image of this mission pop into my mind earlier only because it was near my house?

Suddenly, I felt the Presence very strongly. God *did* want me in this church. God was here, and that comforted me. For the first time, I welcomed God's presence.

RCIA, *Holy Ghost, and That Catholic Stuff*

The liturgy gradually became understandable. Early on, though, I realized that if Old Mission was where God wanted me to keep my promise, I needed to become educated about Catholicism. So, I began attending the Rite of Christian Initiation of Adults (RCIA) classes. Thanks to the priests who led these classes, Fr. Barry and Fr. Herbert, and Marie Cosgrove, who assisted, the puzzle pieces of my life began to lock themselves into a picture I could accept. Complete understanding is yet, if ever, to come. *Ecclesiastes* tells us such understanding is beyond the capacity of even the wisest human. Over time, I have come to accept that God may always remain a mystery to me, that what I receive from God I must take on faith, and that God's grace alone is enough.

At the end of my RCIA year, I was confirmed at the Easter Mass. My daughter-in-law acted as my sponsor. I had had no idea that she was Catholic! Given my outspoken atheism, she had never felt she could discuss spiritual matters with me.

At our last RCIA meeting, which took place after Confirmation, Fr. Herbert asked me about the reception of the Holy Spirit. After all, during the Rite of Confirmation, the priest says, "Receive the seal of the Holy Spirit, the Gift of the Father."

My response disappointed Fr. Herbert: Confirmation was not the time I first encountered the Holy Spirit. I know in Catholic doctrine it is "supposed" to be that way—or maybe we just become aware of the Holy Spirit at that time because of the nature and words of Confirmation—but for me it simply was *not* that way. The Holy Spirit led me *to* Confirmation. Confirmation was a pact between God and me: my public agreement to accept the Divine indwelling and my commitment to follow wherever God led me.

Recently, as I read Fr. Richard Rohr's *The Naked Now*, I found confirmation of my experience with the Holy Spirit. "The divine indwelling<" writes Rohr, "is never earned by any behavior whatsoever or any ritual, but recognized and realized . . . [as] an underlying experience of God as both abyss and ground . . . [an] experience of the Presence that paradoxically always fills the abyss and the ground"—precisely what I experienced as a Divine invasion.

Over time, I have found that while there are patterns in God's behavior that have been noticed by spiritual leaders throughout the centuries and that have formed, informed, and reformed the canons of religions, there is also an arbitrariness to God. God does what God wants with whomever God wants at whatever time God wants. I suppose that is because God *can*.

Why Catholic?

At first, I wondered why God had pushed me in the door of the Catholic Church rather than a mosque (I was living in the Middle East weeks before my conversion), a synagogue (Doah's godfather and the guardian named in our will for our children when they were small are both Jewish), the Orthodox church (the only church in which I had spent any time due to spiritual events in the lives of my many Russian friends), or a Protestant church (considering that I grew up in a WASP community). Over time, I have learned that God knew exactly what I needed: mystic spirituality and spiritual discipline. Both are pervasive attributes of the Catholic Church.

Spirituality

As Rohr and Martos (*Why Be Catholic?*) point out, "Catholic consciousness is a historical consciousness;" the church has a "profound sense of history." Specifically, there is a centuries-old history of exegesis, mysticism, spirituality, and role-modeling of the walk with God, especially among the Franciscans, the founders of Old Mission San Ignatio and the order which keeps our local retreat center. Only with increasing experience have I learned how blessed I was to fall into the hands of the Franciscans.

Discipline

Discipline has turned out to be equally important for this free spirit from the '60s. Although we may rebel against the catechesis of the Church where it does not match our own precepts or makes us uncomfortable about some aspects of our lives, we cannot but admit that the tenets are carefully considered, worked out by faithful believers over many centuries and based on the principles that Jesus gave us. The Catholic Church has put an order to the days and to the hours of our spiritual lives that I find refreshing and comforting. It is indeed a healthy discipline.

I know that there are those who chafe against this discipline of the Catholic Church and second-guess any spiritual authority that might be "over" them. Fr. Thomas Dubay (*Faith and Certitude)* describes them as follows:

> One of the chief reasons some religiously minded people do not en-ter the Catholic Church is that they are not prepared to make the act of faith, that is, the act of submitting their judgment to a liv-ing authority. The problem is not that the evidences for a divine origin of the Church are lacking. On the contrary, they are clear and abundant. What is lacking is the attitude of a mind willing to accept what it does not see simply on the authority of a teacher. These people may profess a great appreciation for Scripture. They may see its beauty, but they are not ready to surrender their belief that their views are superior to another's. They will not bring them-selves to admit that a teacher who contradicts their ideas could be divinely authorized. This is why the root obstacle to faith is pride.

I admit that I could be one of those stubborn ones who would cling to my own ideas above those of others. What stops me is knowing that God put me in the Catholic Church and, for that reason alone, I must accept the teaching of the Church.

There are those, too, who would chafe against the discipline of God for those whom God loves, God disciplines. To react in this way, though, works against our own self-interests and the wishes that God has for us. D. A. Carson (*How Long, O Lord?)*, writes, "If he [God] disciplines those he loves and punishes those he ac-cepts as his children, then to chafe unduly under such punishment is to betray our immaturity—or even, finally, to call into question our desire to grow in conformi-ty to our heavenly Father." *Proverbs* 13:18 states the importance of discipline even more strongly and succinctly: "Whoever disregards discipline comes to poverty and shame, but whoever heeds correction is honored."

Mass

One of the great blessings of Catholic discipline for me has been the daily Mass. Although I am always greedy for as much time as possible with God since I missed out on so many decades, I cannot attend every day. Work requirements preclude that. I do attend whenever I have a day off from work, and I mark Wednesday and Friday noon hours, the days that Mass is celebrated at a chapel near my office, as "do not schedule" on my calendar. My admin assistant tries carefully to keep those times sacred. She succeeds 80% of the time, and my afternoons on those days have a spe-cial feel to them as I bring the Presence that is in the Host back to the office.

Yes, indeed, God knew what He was doing when He pushed me in the door of the Catholic Church. I will be eternally grateful.

Getting Involved

Once inside that door, I found my leisure activities changing. They have become connected with aspects of deepening spirituality, *metanoia*, and with providing assistance to others walking the same path.

Prayer Vigil

Not long after my confirmation, Fr. Herbert needed surgery. The most unlikely candidate possible led the prayer vigil for him the night before the surgery: me. I am a great follower where there are many leaders jumping in to manage a project. At work, I hold a leadership position and therefore lead by default. In the community, however, I am happy to let someone else run things and lend my hands for clean-up chores or other dirty tasks that no one else wants. I don't know why there was no competition to lead the prayer vigil. Given the vacuum, I found myself, a neophyte at prayer, leading the vigil. Blessedly, along came Marie, instructor of my RCIA class, and helped me with the prompts and words. Afterward, I took the candle, which I had placed into a holder I had bought in the Holy Land, from the vigil to the hospital, where I gave it to Fr. Herbert.

Prayer Group

My RCIA education was augmented by discussions at the Old Mission prayer group. At the prayer vigil for Fr. Herbert, the Old Mission prayer group leader invited me to attend the weekly prayer group meetings. Curious as to what a prayer group does, I attended the next meeting and every one after that. There I met Sr. M and a number of other people who have been blessings in my spiritual development and life. It is difficult to say whether the prayer group is a collection of friends or a family. In either case, it is more than a group of individuals gathering weekly for prayer. Grateful for all that I had learned from the other members of the group and especially from the founder-leader, I was saddened to learn that job requirements were taking the leader away from the group and then panicked to learn that he thought I might be a good successor. The former atheist who was still learning the ropes of Catholicism? I didn't think that this was the best idea he had ever had, but, as in so many other cases, what I thought did not matter. I ended up as the prayer group leader—and quickly ran up the hill to our local retreat center and recruited a trained spiritual director to co-lead.

Catechism

Likewise, when the director of religious education asked me (*me?*) to help teach catechism classes, I assured her that she had the wrong person in mind. After all, I was still learning about Catholicism. She assured me that *all* catechists were still learning about Catholicism. The next thing I knew I was teaching teenagers (my favorite age) in the first year confirmation class. The director teamed me with Renee, a cradle Catholic, from whom I have learned much about the workings of the church. Now into my fifth year of assisting Renee, co-teacher and friend, I find that I am still learning. Perhaps the director was right: all catechists continue to learn. Perhaps that is the greatest reward for being a catechist.

Study

I am a scholar by training, career, and in-born nature. My experiences with the prayer group and catechism classes whet my appetite for more learning. "More input; more input!" as Number Five, the robot in the movie, *Short Circuit*, would say. I began to read voraciously, beginning with the old mystics (*The Book of Privy Counseling*, which is my favorite spiritual book of all time, *The Cloud of Unknowing*, Br. Lawrence's *Practice of the Presence of God*). I continued with the works of the renowned Carmelites, St. Teresa of Avila and St. John of the Cross, whose works on locutions and the dark night of the soul, respectively, have elucidated many of my own experiences. I then moved on to read everything I could find by the Franciscans (St. Bonaventure, in particular, and authors reflecting on the life of St. Francis, in general) and every book published by the contemporary Marianist, Fr. Thomas Dubay.

In the process of all this self-teaching and reading, I discovered that Old Mission had a Bible Study group, and I immediately signed up for it. Yes! More input! I received more than just intellectual input and collegial support, however. Soon after I joined the group, I learned that the leader, a long-time Catholic who had converted to Catholicism decades ago from atheism had also experienced a heirophany similar to mine. His period of being caught in the vise of the cosmic nutcracker matched mine exactly: two weeks. Knowing that there are others with similar experiences is faith confirming. I have a feeling that our meeting was not accidental. The leader died unexpectedly last fall. Delaying my required pending business trip, I wrote the intentions at the behest of Sr. M, who had been tasked with organizing that part of the liturgy, and read them at the funeral Mass. Who would have thought?

God's Credit Card

Metanoia affected not only those events and activities associated with the church, but also it permeated all of my life. One area involved how I began to deal with panhandlers and others in need. For years, I have had queasy feelings about giving money to panhandlers, except in those cases where I had the time and cash in hand to invite them to share a meal with me at a nearby restaurant. I disliked the thought of giving to people who did not really need the money or to people who were going to use it to make their condition worse, e.g., buying alcohol with it. Over time, though, I came to the conclusion that true giving is separated from dictating what a person does with the gift. So, that dilemma for me was resolved.

There arose another dilemma, though. I do not carry money with me very often because I have so often been mugged. I do not need to carry money because we are a plastic society, pretty much worldwide these days. So, whenever a panhandler or a person clearly in need crossed my path, I was rarely able to help. Then, I would ask God to give me another chance to help—and would blow it again because I would have only plastic with me and, as usual, it was nearly always maxed out.

On one of those occasions when I was apologizing for missing yet another opportunity to help one of God's people in need into my head popped the concept that God can use plastic, too. And so I got God a credit card.

It was one of those card offers for a small credit line: $250. One can, with time, increase it as the bank and the customer build a relationship, but $250 seemed to be quite an appropriate limit. I reasoned that I would never end up putting that much on the card and that with that limit I could not possibly get in over my head. From then on, I reserved this particular card for God's purposes. Whenever God put someone in need in my path, I would pay with God's credit card.

People in Need

At first, the opportunities to use God's credit card matched my expectations. A couple of examples come to mind:

(1) I met a man in the parking lot of our local grocery store. He was on his way from Ohio to southern California to move in with his daughter, having lost his job in Ohio. He had run out of food money the day before and was hungry. He asked for a couple of dollars for a doughnut and coffee. He thought that would carry him through the remaining six hours of his trip. I told him I had no cash but did have a "special" credit card. If he would pick out what he wanted for lunch and for the road, I would pay for it. So, he did, very judiciously. At the same time, I picked up some strawberries for dessert for dinner for Donnie and me. They were on sale: buy one, get one free. (This kind of sale, just at the right moment, happens so regularly now that I would be surprised if it did not happen.) So, I gave the free strawberries to the hungry man; obviously, the sale was intended for him. As for paying off the credit card bill, the amount was so minor that I was able to include it in our food budget.

(2) One night, about the time that the town was rolling up its sidewalks, I dashed to the grocery store to pick up supper. There, a young couple came up to me, the girl crying, saying that they were out of gas, no one would help them out, and that they were only two hours away from their destination. They looked younger than my kids, and it turns out that they were only 19, traveling across country for the first time to see some childhood friends. They begged for just one gallon of gas, enough to get to a town with more people where they might be able to get more help. I told them that I had no cash and explained about my special credit card. Asking them to fol-

low me to our only gas station, I used the credit card to fill up their tank. They were very grateful and extremely relieved. The cost? $36. The next day, one of our church members saw me at daily Mass. This church member told me that she really needed some copies of my *Blest Atheist* book immediately. (I keep a few books on hand.) Once she had paid me for the books and I had ordered the replacements at author's discount, my "profit" was exactly $36, just enough to pay the credit card bill.

The Limit Increases

I have no doubt that God likes to use that credit card, given the opportunities that arise. I did become a bit worried when the bank automatically raised the limit to $4500. Yikes! What might God have in mind, I wondered? I have not been presented with situations requiring that high an infusion of cash, but I have had situations where the card funded hundreds of dollars, and in one case, $1300, all paid off within a month. How that happens is one of those mysteries I may never figure out.

In one case, when a friend needed an airline ticket for evangelical work in Texas, I was able to get him a first class roundtrip ticket for just $35 and frequent flier miles. I used God's credit card to pay for it. Then I settled down to work on bills since it was payday. As I worked through the budget, I found a $35 bill that I had already paid!

In another case, I had charges of nearly $300 on the card and no particular income in sight. That was before lunch at a local restaurant with a visiting team of scholars from the University of California at Berkeley. The head of the team had wanted to get my input on a grant project. Free lunch with great company at my favorite restaurant constituted excellent payment for an afternoon of idea sharing, I thought. However, as the team was preparing to leave, the admin assistant asked me for my mailing address in order to send me my $500 honorarium!

Mary

"Go dancing tonight," the doctor told me at the end of my appointment. He agreed with me that I have been blessed with better health than my attention to taking care of myself deserved. So, I went dancing. Well, not literally dancing, but the effect was the same.

Donnie and I decided to grab a Subway sandwich and take it back home to San Ignatio, which has no fast food joints. We had some new movies from Netflix and decided that after a hard week we deserved a relaxing evening at home. But first, we were to be given a chance to take care of one of God's children.

Outside Subway, we encountered a girl in her early twenties. As we walked past her, she asked us for a dollar.

"What do you need it for?" I asked. Well, being a mother, I have to *know* some things from kids in their twenties.

"Food," she replied.

Ah, in that case, I had a better solution than a dollar bill. I handed her one of the $10 McDonald cards I carry around for panhandlers asking for a meal when I do not have time to accompany them somewhere where we can use God's credit card. She could buy a couple meals with that. She thanked me and seemed sincere about it.

As Donnie and I stood in line, we had second thoughts. McDonald's was on the other side of town, and here we were at a place selling *food*. For heaven's sake, we could buy her a meal on the spot and not make her trek somewhere else. Then she would have the McDonald's card for the next day.

So, I went back outside to talk to the young lady. She had started to walk off, ostensibly to go to McDonald's. "Excuse me," I called after her. "What's your name?"

She approached me. "Mary," she answered. Now there's a name that makes you think twice!

"Well, Mary, would you let us buy you a meal?" I asked.

She agreed with a wide smile, and in we went. We talked about the kinds of sandwiches we wanted while waiting in line, and she seemed ill at ease. That made sense, I thought. She did not know us. However, the real reason soon came to light.

"I don't know how to ask this," she started, then continued. "I feel guilty about accepting a meal for myself and then going home to my hungry family. I was trying to collect money to buy food for them all. Could I get something for them, too?"

"Of course. How many of them are there?" I asked.

"Six," she responded. "Two children, my mother, my sister, and my brother-in-law, besides me."

"Okay," I told her. "We can manage that." Of course, we could manage that. I had God's credit card.

Mary excused herself briefly to use the bathroom. The lady in front of us in line had overheard everything and suggested that we save money by getting three footlongs cut in half. That way it would only be $15 and would still be enough for six people. I considered it briefly and decided to leave that decision to God. It was, after all, *God's* credit card.

Mary came back just in time to order. She immediately asked for four footlongs and two children's meals. As she darted back and forth between the person handling the bread and meat and the person handling the toppings, I remembered so many times doing the same thing with our kids. Sometimes, I had ordered as many as ten, depending upon who was home at the time. It was always quite an experience for the sandwich makers when my family came to dinner or I stopped by to bring sandwiches home. I got involved in the information passing to the sandwich makers, helping Mary. What joy! What fun! For a brief few minutes, through Mary, I was back with my kids in younger years. The interaction reminded me of what Meister Eckhart said in *Sermon Six*: "People ought to give joy to the angels and the saints. . . Every saint has such great delight and such unspeakable joy from every good work

. . . no tongue can tell, no heart can think how great is the joy they have from this." Watching Mary, I began to understand Meister Eckhart's words.

Finally done, we packed up all the sandwiches, chips, drinks, and headed out the door. "How far do you have to walk?" I asked Mary, eyeing her multiple bags.

"Oh, I live nearby," she said. "Near the dollar store."

"That's more than a mile away!" I protested. "We will drive you."

So, we drove her there, talking along the way about her family, current situation, boyfriend—and the, yikes, fact that she might be pregnant.

"How are you going to feed the baby?" Donnie, now the dad again, probed.

"Well, my boyfriend has agreed to get married. He has a job."

That seems like a backward way to do things, but modern days differ from the days in which we grew up. Nonetheless, both Donnie and I slipped right back into the parent role, discussing the implications of these kinds of things. She accepted our words even though we were not her parents. Somehow, it seemed natural.

All too soon, we arrived and let her out. She started to walk away, then set down her bags and came back to me as I was about to get back into the car after helping her with the bags. She reached out and gave me a big hug and smile.

"Thanks," she said. And that was it.

Indeed, I had followed the doctor's orders. I had gone dancing.

God Reclaims the Card

I admit I can be tempted. While I have been careful to use God's credit card only for those people God places in front of me, I did once encounter an unexpected situation where I ended up reluctantly using God's credit card to pay for Donnie's new computer. He had a chance to get 25% off on a new laptop, which he desperately needed since his desktop computer had stopped work a couple of weeks earlier and his laptop was ten years old. He was dead in the water when it came to doing his work in graphics consulting, and so he had no choice but to find another computer.

Fortunately, a friend had some good connections with Apple and was able to get us a super deal. However, it turned out that we simply did not have the money even for an unimaginably good deal. The only credit card that could cover the nearly four thousand dollar price of a professional computer was God's credit card. I was very reluctant to use it. I do not use it for personal needs, but if we did not use it at this point, Donnie would be without work for a long while. Moreover, the special deal was available only on the day we were offered it. Sighing, I agreed to use God's credit card, feeling considerably guilty. I mentally calculated the length of time it would take me to pay off the card. That did not reassure me at all.

After paying for the computer, I went to the post office. In the mail box was a new credit card from a bank I had not used in twenty years but to which I still belonged. The bank wanted me back as a customer. The credit line was the same as on

God's credit card! I would be able to transfer the balance without any interest for a year. I immediately activated the card, transferred the balance, and God's credit card was once again cleared for God's purposes.

That was stunning: God rescued the credit card from my illicit use! I know now that I must keep that card clear for God's purposes—and people in need are sent my way routinely. There is no doubt that this particular credit card belongs to God.

Prodigality

I would be remiss if I were to present the *metanoias* I experience as a straight line, upward spiral, or any kind of algebraic or geometric progression. There are also slides backward. Old habits die slowly. There are times when I forget that everyone has a God-seed inside, no matter how difficult it may be to see it. Let me share one experience of which I am *not* proud.

Bad Start

I don't know where the words came from. Even as I heard them, I could hardly believe they were coming from my mouth.

"I don't think you are taking this project seriously," I said to a project manager at our Washington D. C. branch. She cringed and averred differently. I only shook my head unkindly and walked off to begin the presentation I had come to deliver.

I can explain how I got to the point of saying those words, but I cannot justify saying them. In preparing for an all-day briefing to be conducted together with one of our specialists, I discovered that the concept papers we were to use were so poorly done that we could not use them. So, I had to re-do the work of several employees, whose supervisor had assumed that the work was fine. To worsen matters, the computers had been down for the two days prior to my departure. I had only one day to get everything done once the computers were back on line. That day I had several meetings, and during my limited available time, one after another employee came into my office on small issues (well, important issues to them but ones I considered minor). Although I had closed my door, no one had seemed to notice. My open-door policy had been turned into an open-the-door policy. Too much to re-do, too little time to re-do it, and too many distractions! I was annoyed.

Add to the annoyance the fact that everyone around me seemed to be falling apart. I had one senior manager undergoing emergency surgery and another in the hospital with internal bleeding. Yet another employee had gone into the hospital for routine knee surgery and ended up comatose and packed in ice, and a junior manager had been diagnosed with a tumor while on a field assignment and had to return. This was all in the space of two days. Our senior leadership at the annual BBQ was decimated. I was stressed.

I did not escape any drama by leaving town. As the plane was taxiing into Dulles International Airport, I checked my Blackberry and learned two disturbing pieces of information. First, one of my projects had been downsized, and the performance date had been moved back a month, creating a conflict with another trip. Second, my supervisor had overturned an appointment I had made to a deserving employee. I was disappointed.

Following a night of only five hours of sleep after cleaning up from the BBQ, which had been at my house, and having had to go to work earlier than normal to begin that day of meetings and interrupted work, I had to jump onto a redeye from San Francisco to DC. Of all times, the pilot raced across the continental skies, arriving 30 minutes ahead of schedule, leaving me with a mere four hours of sleep. I was tired.

When I arrived at ground transportation, I blackberried the supervisor of our DC branch for an address. She gave me the office address. I showed up there only to find out that the briefing was taking place in another part of town. Now I would be late. I learned that the mistaken address was deliberate: the supervisor first wanted to discuss the project with me alone. That meant that the specialist, who did not have the briefing power points (I had them), would have to do the first presentation without them and without me. I was angry.

Annoyance, stress, fatigue, disappointment, and anger combined to evoke my caustic remark when, having arrived at the right location in time for the second presentation, I was informed by the project manager that two key personnel would come only after lunch. Any one of those conditions would have served as an excuse for my remarks, I told myself. However, no justification exists for arrogance, and it was arrogance that lay behind my words: whatever I had to say was more important than anything they had to do. Obviously, that was not true.

I apologized to the project manager later. However, words don't dissolve; they don't run away; taking them back can occur only metaphorically.

I was not *thinking* of God's presence when I made my unkind remark. So, I did not *feel* God's presence. The worst part? I lost an entire morning with God. That time will never be regained.

Clearly, I needed some time with God alone. After finishing the day of presentations, I ran to the nearby metro station where I knew there would be a line of cabs to assist me in my cab-plane-car dash to our Georgia branch, my next stop. I grabbed a cab, driven by a courteous and calm middle-aged man from Pakistan. We chatted casually, and while the conversation was calming, it, too, permitted no opportunity for time alone with God. I missed San Ignatio with its quiet spirituality.

At the Airport

Once at the airport, I swiftly picked up my ticket and passed through security without incident except for my usual "random" selection to be searched. I then took the airport train to the Delta terminal and made my way to Gate 76, keeping my eye out for any place for quiet prayer. There was none, just masses of people moving in cohorts to and from gates, into and out of restrooms and restaurants, and along the corridors. I missed even more San Ignatio where nearly every nook and cranny provides an opportunity for prayer.

I had more than an hour to wait for a delayed plane. I opted for a yogurt cone and seated myself at a table near a large potted plant, surrounded, of course, by other travelers.

My thoughts turned to my increasing unease. From where were these feelings coming? A change in the equilibrium of my life! I realized that I spend most of my time helping others, sometimes because I have been given a divine task, sometimes just because I stumble across someone in need, and most often because those in need are people who work for me. My last few days, however, had been focused on me: the just-completed presentations in DC and the upcoming one in Georgia. I had moved away from helping others for lack of time (the employees to whom I had shut my door), lack of authority (the overturning of my decision by my supervisor), and lack of ability (the sick folks). I missed helping others, being God's helper. I missed time with God. It would be two more days before I would return to San Ignatio.

Even though I had no sense of God's presence while I waited for the plane, I wailed a silent prayer, spilling out all these emotions and desires. I knew God would hear, understand, and forgive. I wailed, too, that I missed San Ignatio and wished so much that I could be there, where time and place with God is easy to find.

And then everything changed. Delta cancelled the flight. There were no other flights on Delta that night. I would miss the Georgia presentation, scheduled for early in the morning the next day. I called my admin assistant to inform the folks in Georgia as Delta set about rescheduling all its passengers.

"Does anyone speak Russian?" one of the gate agents called out loudly, then a few seconds later, appealed again, "We really need someone who speaks Russian."

"I'll call you back," I told my admin assistant. Then I stood up and raised my hand, "I speak Russian."

The gate agent was visibly relieved. So were the mother and daughter who were trying to get back to Moscow via Atlanta. We easily settled everything for them, and as their stress level eased, so did mine. I find that happens a lot—if you help someone who is stressed out, it eases your own feeling of stress.

The grateful Delta agent offered to take me out of turn, but I turned down the offer, telling her that my office could handle my situation. It did. Since I would miss the presentation opportunity, there was no sense in continuing on to Georgia. I ended up coming back to San Ignatio early on a United non-stop flight direct to San Francisco. What could be better? How about a surprise complimentary upgrade to first class, a reward for having flown nearly 150,000 miles that year on United? Another redeye, but one on which I could sleep very comfortably.

All was right with the world. I was on my way back to San Ignatio. I wondered how much of this occurred because of my plaintive prayer about missing my quiet time with God. Ah, for any—and every—part of it, I was grateful.

Spoiled by God

Looking back on that awful day and what I had done and felt, I should have been punished. Instead, a loving God brought me home to San Ignatio, back to God in every meaning of that phrase, back to where I belong, where nothing of the material world matters.

I took the next day off from work—I was owed comp time—to be with God now that I was back in a spiritual environment. What a marvelous day that turned out to be, especially since that evening began a four-day retreat, from the first evening of which I had been exempted because of having to be in Georgia.

Immediately upon arising on my morning off, I checked my email. Astonished, I read one note twice. It was the cancellation of a mandatory meeting on Friday, the second day of the retreat, from which the retreat leader had also excused me. Even though I had planned to redeye back from Georgia Thursday evening, I still had to be at that all-day meeting on Friday. This note, along with my early return, would allow me to attend the entire retreat—and, certainly, I needed that retreat!

A short while later, I attended noon Mass in the little chapel that is attached to Old Mission. Following Mass, two friends asked me to join them for the rosary, after which we went out for coffee and milk. (They had coffee; I had milk, an unremarkable favorite for a former farm girl.) I told my friends about my plaintive prayer, in which I had bemoaned my separation from San Ignatio and loss of a sense of God's presence in the tumult of the past few days, and how everything had suddenly worked out for me to spend the entire rest of the week with God. One of my friends reiterated what a Sufi friend told me several years ago, word for word: "God spoils you."

Indeed, God does! I am so very grateful!

Surround Sound

When *Inception* first came out, Donnie and I decided to go to the theater, which is a very infrequent activity for us, to watch this raved-about movie. It did turn out to be an entertaining film, but it was not the movie that riveted my attention.

Donnie bought the typical snack foods. I picked up a hot dog because I had not had a chance to eat earlier that day. I added to that order an icee. That was my nourishment for the day. It was not the best, but also not the worst, I could have chosen.

Since there were only a handful of people at the theater, an unfortunate sign of the difficult economic times in 2010, we settled into the best seats in the house.

The trailers of upcoming movies played through, and *Inception* started. By then, I had already finished my meal. I had been hungry enough to gulp down the icee and finish the hot dog in three bites. I put down the empty containers and prepared to watch the movie.

Soon, though, I realized that I was only half-watching. For some reason, the longer I sat there, the stronger the presence of God became until it seemed like we had another person in the theater with us. It remained that way throughout the movie. It was the loveliest, most comforting feeling. Although movies of this type usually cause my adrenaline to rush, as they are meant to do, I felt nothing of the sort with this one. The longer I sat there together with God, the calmer I became even as the suspense and action in the movie was reaching a crescendo.

When we left the theater, I was very relaxed and calm, almost in a stupor. As in the case of contemplative prayer, with which this experience had much in common, I did not want to leave, but, of course, I had to. It was as if I had been in two places at the same time, doing two things at the same time. It was simultaneous contemplation (this sitting together with God) and action (the thrills of the movie).

For me, the experience underscored that God is always with me; just sometimes I can sense God's presence more than other times. Perhaps it was meant to be a lesson always to keep in mind and know that even in the busiest moment I can communicate with God if I want to. Or perhaps it was simply a gift. I like to think that God just wants to give me a present of Presence upon occasion, the best gift one could ever receive.

Contemplation

I came to God through a hierophany, a term derived from Greek for *holy* (*hieros*) and *bringing to light* (*phainein*) and probably first used by religious historian Mircea Eliade to indicate a breaking through of the sacred into the profane. Following the grace that opened my life to the Presence of God and the subsequent two weeks in which I wrestled with the sense of an invading Presence, I remained with God and grew in understanding primarily through contemplative prayer although initially I did not even know the term for what I was experiencing. I certainly did not realize that generally contemplation is a state one reaches after a long spiritual journey.

Contemplation, according to the *Catechism of the Catholic Church*, is a "gaze of faith" and a "silent love." It is through contemplation that one experiences union with God. The Desert Fathers, hermits who lived in the Scetes Desert in Egypt during the third century, were the first to describe contemplation, labeling it *hesychasm* (Greek: stillness, silence) and describing it as a prayer of the heart characterized by interior silence (see, e.g., *Philokalia* by Abba Philimon).

In *Benjamin Major*, Richard of St. Victor, a mystic in the 1100s, defines contemplation as taking the human mind beyond its practice of reason and rationality to a state of complete self-surrender to God. In this state, a person is "radiant with infused heavenly light and lost in wonder at the supreme beauty of God," "torn from the foundation of her being so that she no longer thirsts *for* God but *into* God."

St. Teresa of Avila later describes contemplation as a "sensation of absorption, fusion, and immersion." Viewing the soul "as if it were a castle made of a single diamond, in which there are many rooms, just as in Heaven there are many mansions," St. Teresa in *Interior Castle* describes seven rooms, or mansions, each representing a deeper level of prayer and through each of which one must pass before reaching the innermost sanctum, a place of complete transfiguration and communion with God.

Contemplation was the means through which God had chosen to communicate with me, to form me, to unite with me, to direct me. The concepts of contemplation, union, and St. Teresa's interior mansions I learned much later, after I had personally experienced them. Thanks to knowledgeable friends and kindly priests, I was pointed in the direction of the old mystics, in whom I found kindred spirits. Thanks to the works of the old mystics, I understood that I was probably not approaching insanity but rather was being given an incredible blessing: Presence that has permeated every cell of my being until I can no longer ascertain where I stop and God begins.

Emptying

Long before I knew anything about God, I learned how to empty myself in ways that would one day open me up for being filled by God through infused contemplation. What caused this learning to happen? Migraines! Seriously!

In 1980, I broke my back. How that occurred was far from exotic. It was, in fact, about as mundane a happening as it could possibly be. While hurrying to get a pair of socks for my three-year-old son Shane, I fell down a flight of stairs. The details of the drama of getting to the hospital instead of going to work that day would fill many pages, so I shall leave that information for another venue. Instead, I will explain what happened after I had spent three months in a body brace to allow my back to heal.

Once out of the brace and back to work, I found myself plagued by migraines. Debilitating, usually preceded by an aura of approaching unavoidable illness, these headaches forced me into bed for a day or more. With four children, a job, and graduate school, not to mention my volunteer activities as an outdoors counselor for the Girl Scouts, I simply could not afford this much time away from life. Yet, the more I forced myself to move beyond the migraines, the more they reached out and pulled me back.

They were intensified, I found through monitoring my daily behavior, by chocolate. I gave up chocolate, but the migraines continued to plague me. Chocolate simply made them appear for certain.

I sought help from a neurologist. The doctor prescribed post-aura medicine. However, I suddenly did not need it.

Before filling the prescription, I had a few more migraines and noticed something peculiar. The more I tried to ignore the headaches, the stronger they became. The more I thought about them, the longer they lasted. The more I tried to work through and past them, the more persistent they grew. On the other hand, the more I gave in to them, embraced them, accepted them, and stopped thinking about anything at all, just relaxing into the migraine, the weaker they became. Perhaps "relaxing" is not the precise word any more than it is the most appropriate word to describe "relaxing" into labor pains or into the pain that accompanies root canals without anesthesia. However, essentially, one goes *with* the pain in all these cases, not *against* it.

I noticed that as I was giving into the pain, I was not thinking about anything. I was simply in a state of unmonitored being, The pain was around me; I was in it and part of it. Eventually, I learned how to put myself into that state instantly at the first ray of an aura. Within seconds, the aura would disappear, and the migraine would not come. The doctor called it biofeedback. I called it emptying my mind.

Shutting down my thinking and just being in the moment has given me 30 migraine-free years. The momentary shutdown is never noticed by anyone I am with because it requires less than two seconds to rebalance my system. I am no doctor, but I have studied the research available on migraines and believe that normal blood flow is restored by my autonomous system during those couple seconds.

Similarly, I stumbled upon a wonderful application of this mind-emptying ability to contemplation. When my mind is empty, there is room for God to enter completely. I cannot meditate; I have tried. Meditation fills my mind, and no sooner than

I start trying to fill it than I feel removed from God. So, my soul, which seems at times to operate independently of my brain, takes over and empties my mind, allowing me to enter that non-thinking, non-acting, just-being state where I can simply "relax" into God and God can "relax" into me.

I suppose it is nigh onto sacrilegious to compare contemplation with migraine reduction, but the experience of one did give me an understanding of the experience of the other. For that reason, I hope God will forgive me my dollop of sacrilege. With the migraine-related mind emptying, I experience only emptiness and after a few seconds re-emerge into a state of action, i.e. my daily life, which is more attractive than the empty state. In periods of contemplation, I experience fullness and even after many minutes, or, when I have the luxury of time, an hour or more, I avoid re-emergence into a state of action, which is less attractive than the contemplative state. The first kind of emptying brings me relief, depends upon me, and every experience is reliably the same. The second kind of emptying brings bliss, and its nature (even its occurrence) is dependent on God, not upon me, and differs each time.

I do not feel that my words are sufficient to articulate the attributes of an extraordinary state that defies ordinary description. The mystics have tried and have certainly done a better job than I. Still, when one talks with those friends who set aside daily time for contemplation, there is something so unique about each incident that the narrating of it differs.

Jesus told his disciples not to tell some of the out-of-the-ordinary things they experienced. I think Bible scholars generally assume this command to mean that if the disciples told, they would not be understood and moreover they themselves might misinterpret the experience. I worry about that whenever I write down the word, *contemplation*, whenever I consider talking or writing about the topic. I am past the point of concern that others might consider me insane, but I doubt that I will ever be past the point of concern that writing down my experience somehow vulgarizes it. I write for my own sanity and recall in some cases and because I am directed to do so in other cases. I also write because, like David, I simply must sing God's praises in the only way I know how, using the gift God has given me: the written word.

Contemplative Prayer

I have found some validation of my experiences in Fr. Richard Rohr's book, *Simplicity*. He also describes contemplative prayer as beginning with emptying. "Jesus went into the wilderness," Rohr writes, "ate nothing for forty days and made himself empty."

Thomas Merton, too, in *An Invitation to the Contemplative Life*, talks about the need for emptiness, which, he contends, is a "most important discovery in the interior life." According to Merton and in my own experience, this emptiness is not a vacuum but an abundant fullness and infinite depth.

From Emptying to Contemplation: The Key Ingredient

"Emptiness in and of itself," Rohr writes, "is not enough. The point of emptiness is that we get ourselves out of the way, so that Christ can fill us up."

Then he points out something that I have found personally to be key. "We don't choose Christ," he continues. "Christ chooses us; he decides for us. As soon as we are empty, there is a place for Christ."

This is why it is difficult for me to describe my experiences. How do you describe something that you do *not* do? Something to which you, emptied, surrender? In *Psalm* 46:10, the Israelites are told, "Be still, and know that I am God." Emptying is a way of becoming still, spiritually quiescent, even weak-willed, so that God's presence and will can take over.

I once looked up this psalm in a Hebrew-English dual-language translation. The Hebrew word used, *raphah*, according to the translator, means to become slack or let go. If we cannot let go, if we cannot surrender our self-control, how can God take control of us?

The key ingredient, then, in my experience is nothingness. Doing nothing. Thinking nothing. Organizing nothing. Asking nothing. Praying nothing. Saying nothing. Just letting go, i.e. being still, and in the stillness, suddenly, there is God.

Night Prayer

Nighttime is the sweetest part of the day for me. I fall into a delicious bed after a supercharged day and let the battery totally drain. Time for prayer! That is the reason for the sweetness. Not that I haven't prayed throughout the day. Indeed, I have. Some days I pray very consciously. Other days I pray more frequently simply by taking notice of God's presence and sharing my life and experiences of the moment with God as one would with Someone who is one's best friend, parent, and lover all rolled into one Entity.

At night, as in the early morning, though, my attention is undivided. Also, unlike during the day when I alternate pleas for guidance with exclamations of gratitude, I have little to say at night. In fact, I usually feel like I am cheating in some way. Instead of a litany of formal prayers that I have yet to learn well enough to pronounce them all by myself, I simply enunciate words of gratitude, ask for grace and mercy for those for whom I have promised (or feel prompted) to pray, beg briefly for my dreams to center only on good and on God, and then fall silent, relaxing in God's pervasive presence, sinking into God's soft love, like a long-married couple gently swinging together on the porch as the night settles around them.

From that quick-to-arrive point of profound comfort, I turn all communication and its direction over to God. I become a listener. As much as I would like to stay awake forever, held in that merciful and loving embrace, I inexorably drift into sleep like a gently rocked baby immersed in a lullaby.

Indeed, I do feel like I am cheating. I don't intone any mantra to induce a state of meditation but slip easily into a contemplative state by letting God do all the work. I don't sit in the "right" position that I have been taught; typically, I don't sit at all. I don't spend specific amounts of time *doing* specific things or saying specific prayers. Proper or not, the end of my day has arrived, and with my duties (and battery) discharged, I don't want to be in control of anything, including myself. So whether or not I am cheating, not following "the system," or breaking the rules on some level, I don't care. If God wants me to follow the rules, I assume God will let me know what those rules are. Until God does that, I intend selfishly to let God do all the work and just rest/sleep on God's bosom.

Faithful Practice

I marvel at how contemplation, practiced faithfully, can, like nearly anything that is practiced faithfully, become routine. It used to be that each morning I would try to remain in a state of quiet prayer for 20-30 minutes before going to work. The hardest part was leaving that perfect moment to go busily about preparing to depart.

Not that God wasn't with me in the preparation. Of course, God was, and I felt God's presence. It was just somehow different and somewhat less satisfying than spending lazy minutes together with God. Being lazy with God is my favorite activity, yet one that I found myself doing less often than I would like.

So, every morning for a while I would try to allow enough time between waking and leaving to begin my day being lazy with God, and every evening before returning I would do the same. Day after day, even when traveling, I wove these lazy times into my schedule although I have to admit that, especially when in travel status, there were days I would miss.

Then something extraordinary happened. I don't know when the change came. I just noticed that it had. I no longer had to plan this time or to remind myself to take the time. It just happened. It had become habit. At least, that's what my detail-oblivious mind first thought. Then I paid closer attention to what was happening.

The contemplative periods had moved away from my control. They were more than habitualized, autonomous responses to the ticking of a clock or the perception of a biorhythm. They were—and are—out of my control and under the control of God. I began waking up a half-hour or more before the alarm in a contemplative state, in the presence of God, and I had no real idea how long we had been being lazy together as morning took over what might have been an all-night joint adventure for I do not remember my dreams.

I know the common wisdom is to practice contemplation sitting in a chair so as not to fall asleep, but since I can fall asleep in any position, even standing, that advice helps me little. So, I go to bed while not tired so that I can spend time in contemplation and then fall asleep in the arms of God. I like to think those arms hold me all night and gently rock me awake in the morning to the joy of being in the presence of God.

Whatever the explanation—I don't need to know why things happen—such a marvelous beginning to the day brings light and happiness to the rest of my day. That continues until some highly stressful, distressing event over which I have no control sends me to the nearest prayer place, i.e. any place I can be alone again with God.

This condition I find myself in, this walking with God, relaxing with God, and desperately looking for God when I stray, became clear to me during a recent retreat. We were given specific instructions and time for contemplation, early morning and late evening not being among them, but God maintained the routine, greeting me in the morning and tucking me into bed at night. How much more blessed can anyone be, I wonder with gratitude so deep I don't know how to express it. The thing that makes the gratitude even sweeter and deeper is that I don't have to know how to express it. I don't have to be able to find all the right words. God knows fully that which I can express only in part.

Who Was Connie?

Last year, I participated in a contemplative prayer group in a nearby city. The group met regularly once a month in the evening. To the last meeting I took a member of our Old Mission prayer group, the difference in the two groups being that the city group was focused on contemplative prayer, leading to very quiet meetings, and our local group is focused on pray-aloud prayer, leading to noisy and inspirational chaos. Both groups included sharing of personal experience and spiritual growth.

The contemplative group always began with paired discussion about the state of our personal prayer life. Then, following a scripture reading, 20 minutes (which never seemed enough) was allotted to contemplative prayer. After that, we usually sang some songs before parting.

During the last session, I was paired with a newcomer, named Connie. Shabbily clothed, with downcast eyes and meek demeanor, Connie looked like she had wandered into the wrong group, most of us being middle-class yuppie types, at least to the common eye. None of us had any idea how she found us or why she had come. She did not want to discuss prayer life during our pair time. Rather, she wanted to talk to me about dying. Connie was in Stage 4 of esophageal cancer, something I know little about except what Connie told me. Spiritual growth was not her concern. Putting closure to her life was. She did not want my advice. That was good for I had none to give. She wanted only a friend. She wanted to be touched, held, hugged— all without words, a difficult task for an extrovert such as I, but I did my best. I said little because I needed to say little. She said anything I would have said and far more. I wish I had listened with my memory as well as my ears because I would like to remember more than I do. I recall that she said that she was ready to die, worried about nothing, and wished only that the pain could be less. She said that she knew that God loved her and added "more than you could possibly understand right now." That was odd, but I did not remonstrate. I just knew I was supposed to listen. She said she had no relatives or real friends in the world, that few would miss her. She accepted that. She wanted nothing before she died, but she did whisper one thing with some urgency before we were called back into a group for our contemplative prayer session: "Pray for me."

During the prayer session, Connie sat in the pew in front of me. What I loved about these prayer sessions was the fading of the external world, the loss of outside distractions, and a sense of union with God. After a short while, however, I felt something happening in the pew in front of me and, suddenly quite aware of all my surroundings, I noticed Connie. She was not praying. She was looking around, and, I swear, she did not look like herself. Not shabby anymore. A softness surrounded her. I could not tell whether it was coming from within or from without, but whatever it was felt holy, even sacred. I blinked several times, thinking I was somehow in a heretofore unexperienced state or at least never-before-described-to-me contemplation, but no, my eyes reported the same odd, holy softness with each blink.

Suddenly Connie stood up, looking much like herself again, and started to walk out. I stood as she passed me and reached out to her with a questioning look. "Good-bye," she said. Nothing more.

"I will pray for you," I promised in a whisper. We embraced warmly, and she walked out.

I could not concentrate after that and sat quietly, waiting for the others to finish praying. Then came our group sing-along of fairly short duration, followed by an announcement about the dissolution of the group. (The priest who led it had recently been reassigned, and we had carried on for a few meetings on our own.) Perhaps it was the sense of imminent personal loss in the group disbandment that kept anyone from noticing that Connie had left. Whatever the reason, no one said a word about it. The prayer group leader dismissed us for the last time. I interrupted before people scattered and asked if anyone had noticed Connie's departure. No one had paid attention to the fact that we were one less in number at the end than at the beginning.

"We don't know who she is," one person said.

"We've never seen her before," another volunteered.

"Perhaps she realized she was in the wrong place," yet another suggested.

Maybe any of those things. Maybe all of those things. Maybe none of those things. I told the group what I knew about Connie (except for the strange vision I had had of her during prayer). I told them about her request for prayer. Instinctively, with no one individual taking the lead, we all formed a circle to pray for Connie. The leader looked at me, and I said what I hoped were adequate words.

I have many times since wondered what happened there. The person from our mission prayer group who had attended with me said that she got the same feeling from Connie that I had: otherworldly, but she had no idea why. Perhaps when one is close to death, one is especially close to God.

Br. Charles, in his Internet blog, *Praise and Bless*, posted a homily that brought Connie back into focus for me. He was addressing the question of transsubstantiation, but I am taking some of his words here out of context because they immediately made me think of Connie:

> When God reveals himself to the world, what appears? On the one hand a newborn, vulnerable child, born of young, poor parents away from home. On the other hand, God reveals himself as a condemned criminal, tortured and in the midst of his execution. These are the mysteries of the Nativity and the Passion, . . . and they reveal a God who is sublimely humble.

Could God have been there in Connie, a humble, dying-from-cancer, living-alone, sixty-something, raggedly clothed, obviously poor, weak woman? A reminder to us that whom we consider "the least" among us may not be the least at all? None of us who were there will probably ever know, but at the time and now thinking back, that sense of another dimension that surrounded Connie still gives me pause.

Who was Connie? Does it matter? At the very least, she was someone who needed support, and we gave the best we could. Isn't that what God wants us to do on this journey we call life?

Death

Connie certainly has died by now. In fact, several people I know have died since my conversion. I found that with their deaths, as with consideration of my own, much has changed. I look at death in a very different way now: as a commencement, not an ending, as merely a change in state and a new life. Whenever Sister Death, to use St. Francis's appellation, comes to visit me, she will be welcomed, not because I have any desire to see her right away but because she is very much a part of this adventure God has granted us to live out.

Goodnight, God!

Last fall, Doah stayed with us for several weeks, sleeping on our couch. One night I spent time on the couch beside him, perseverating on computer work until the wee hours of the morning. I could see him drifting off to sleep as his breathing slowed. Right before he totally zonked out, I heard him whisper, "Goodnight, God." Then he was unwakeably asleep for the rest of the night.

As a child, Doah would make a nest of blankets under my desk and sleep there. As a mentally challenged child, he did not think of the world in the same terms as those around him, and I always wondered what his teachers might think of us as parents if he told them that he slept in a nest! Since Doah's nesting days. I have not observed him falling asleep. So, I was unaware that he always says goodnight to God.

As I watched him, I realized how much we can learn from the simplicity of mentally challenged individuals. He seems to have a direct link to God. There is no evident barrier—you know, the kinds of barriers we throw up between ourselves and God so that we can avoid getting too close.

Doah often says, "God told me this, or God told me that." I take his words at face value. I do not know how otherwise to react to them.

I remember Doah's reaction when I first moved to San Ignatio, where one feels that the town itself is holy. (One of my Russian Orthodox friends, a very devout believer, turned to me on her first visit as we were walking around town and said, "Beth, etot gorodok namolein," the closest translation of which would be "this town is soaked in prayer.") Doah stood at my stoop, looked around, turned around a time or two, then faced me, and proclaimed, "God here."

In all our efforts at prayer, our attempts to live as God would have us live, to open ourselves to God, I wonder if we ever consider that developing a relationship with God might be as simple as Doah sees it—just allowing oneself to be together with God as one would be together with a friend, noticing that "God here," and remembering to say "good night, God." I now say "good night, God" every night when I feel myself drifting off to sleep, following a period of contemplative prayer. Equally important, every morning upon rising, my first words now are "Good morning, God."

Manifestations

If the palpable presence of God unnerved me, the visions and locutions that have followed at irregular intervals have overwhelmed me. Initially, I assumed that all the converted experienced these phenomena. Over time, I found that if all the converted do experience them, all the converted are not aware of them.

So, over time I have silenced my urges to share my experiences, assuming that the response I will get is a raised eyebrow at best and a reputation as crazy at worst. I suppose this concerns me because there is a part of all of us that wants to appear sane. There is also a part of me that upon occasion questions the authenticity of my experiences and my own sanity.

On the other hand, there are things that lead me to question the consistency of those who would naysay my experiences. Why do we sing "Open my eyes that I may see visions of truth Thou hast for me" if we do not accept a reality in which images appear unto us? Likewise, why do we sing "Open my ears that I may hear voices of truth Thou sendest clear" or "I come to the garden alone…and the voice I hear falling on my ear the son of God discloses" if we do not accept a reality in which a voice comforts, guides, and tasks us? "We live as if God has quit speaking to his people," Blackaby and King (*Experiencing God*) assert. "God clearly spoke to His people in *Acts*. . . . God has not changed. He still speaks to His people."

For now, where the experiences do not contradict scripture, I take them at face value and wait until I can find a way to interpret them. If someone appears who can provide an explanation, I listen. If I can determine the authenticity of a tasking, I complete it. If I cannot, I wait. I assume that in time God will reveal what it is I should know. The rest is unimportant.

Light on the Path

I have come to associate light with God. One experience in particular served to reinforce that association. I had attended the Sunday noon Mass at Old Mission, which was conducted in Spanish by a visiting priest, so perhaps I had not understood something. The priest had spent missionary time abroad and had not liked the foreign people—their customs differed from American customs, and, therefore, they were, in his opinion, wrong. Wrong, too, were Protestants, Muslims, Jews, and other non-Catholics. God loved only Catholics. At least, that is what I understood him to say. I certainly hope that I misunderstood for we know from Jesus' words and actions that God loves all of creation.

The homily distressed me. After the Mass, I fumed up and down the blackberry-lined path that runs behind our mission. On the one hand, who was I to judge the priest? On the other hand, did not God send disciples to Jews and Gentiles alike? And then there are atheists like I had been. I have pretty strong evidence that during my decades of atheism God loved me in spite of my atheism. It seems to me, then, that God loves all of us, regardless of gender, race, ethnicity, religious denomination (i.e. whether we get all the pieces of spirituality "right" or not), and even level of faith. That is ubiquitous and unconditional love. So, how could the priest state that only Catholics are worthy of God's love? Hating those who differ from you doesn't make the world a better place any more than hating your personal enemy makes your own life any better. God's message is about love and inclusion, not about power, position, territory, and domination. So, when we do start praying for our enemies and not only for our families and friends?

I often walked along that path after Sunday Mass, picking blackberries and talking to tourists. That day, though, I walked down an unusually deserted path, still distressed enough from the homily not even to wonder where the tourists might be.

How could a priest say such things? I wondered. I had been attending Old Mission for only about six weeks and had not yet realized that priests are human beings. I still had much to learn about Catholicism—or any brand of organized religion, for that matter. I had yet to learn that God's grace by itself is sufficient.

Suddenly, I realized that I was fully alone. Not only were there no other people on the path, but also I could not sense God's presence. That made the whole morning unacceptably disturbing.

"Where are You?" I asked. There was no answer.

"Where are you?" I asked again, plaintively, and this time quite loudly.

The answer came quietly, "I am with you."

I did not feel God with me, perhaps because of the invasion of negative emotions that came from my reaction to the visiting priest's homily. So, I repeated the question with some frustration, "Where *are* You?"

I heard the same quiet response, "I am with you."

Still, I felt nothing. So, I wailed, "I don't *feel* You with me!"

At that moment, a near-blinding light enveloped the blackberry bushes, the path, me, and, seemingly, the entire world. Time stopped as in a science fiction movie except that it was real, or at least real to me. For perhaps 30 seconds, I was totally immobilized by this overwhelming light that carried within itself a sense of tremendous power. I understood that this was just a fraction of the potential power that could have been directed at me. I immediately decided never to ask for that kind of proof again, and I am now very careful in general as to what I ask for (because I often get it). I am clearly in over my head with God; there is so much for me to learn.

When the light "released" me, I asked for an explanation of the priest's commentary, but none came. I picked and ate the blackberries along the path without paying much attention to what I was doing until my hands were stained purple on both sides and somewhat torn by thorns. At one point, I sat down in the brambles, out of sight, and kept praying for an explanation. None came. (But I did later end up with a bad case of poison oak in unscratchable places.)

I walked on, up over the hill. As I walked, I realized that I had received an answer, from where I do not know, perhaps just from an implanted thought, an important one: God cannot be judged by the words or behaviors of people. Tangential to that, I realized that I didn't require an explanation because I was at peace with the understanding that God's grace in and of itself is sufficient. I stopped in the shadow of one of the great old olive trees at the end of the path and finally was able to respond, "It is enough that You are with me."

The Voice

Locutions without images have been the most common forms of my encounters with God. Locutions I receive are always on God's terms and at God's times. I cannot prompt them, nor would I want to do that for they usually unnerve me. Typically, they come in the middle of something else. Each remains seared into my memory because of the element of surprise and the content of the message, which is always something I do not want to hear or do.

It has taken a considerable amount of time for me to learn that locutions are a rare gift. Everything in my conversion came along topsy-turvy. I did not run begging to God for help nor did I seek God in any way. I was a chronically happy atheist. My world did not shatter, and God did not lift me from among the shards. My world was a place of joy.

Because I did not come to God through the church but rather to the church through God, contemplative prayer, my starting point, is to this day much easier for me than the prayers that most Catholics have known since childhood. I am still trying to learn these beautiful traditional prayers and have given up on ever knowing all those that cradle Catholics know. I still have trouble with the mysteries part of the rosary and need a cheat sheet or someone to prompt me. Talking to God, on the other hand, comes easily, and listening to God comes even more easily.

Clearly, I am making judgments based on a backward journey from communication and contemplation to formal ritual. Nonetheless, I share experiences with a number of other people. Among them is a dear Sufi friend who taught me the Arabic word, *zikr*, used by the Sufis for what I experience. I have to wonder, it being my nature to wonder, if there would not be more people who receive locutions if they truly believed that God wants to communicate with us. Just as most people find that a difficult thing to believe, I find the opposite difficult to believe. Why would God create people and then go silent?

While I usually perceive the locutions as coming from an external voice, they are probably interior in nature, following St. Teresa of Avila's description of them. Our brains are marvelously complex organs, so marvelous that even the greatest expert in cognitive neuroscience comes close to understanding only a fraction of its functions. I suspect that my brain takes liberties with my auditory faculties and synaptic processing, cross-wiring them, which makes me think I have heard something spoken aloud rather than interiorly, "words heard more clearly than with the ears," to cite St. Teresa.

My greatest fear is that the words of any particular locution may have been sent not by the Divine but by the Sinister. To distinguish the latter from the former, I rely upon St. Teresa's description of the difference in her diary (published later as *The Life of St. Teresa by Herself*). The Divine gifts produce quietude, whereas the Sinister produce disquietude. "This disquietude," wrote St. Teresa, " is such that I know not whence it comes: only the soul seems to resist, is troubled and distressed, without knowing why; for the words of Satan are good, and not evil." Her descriptions help me immensely in separating the ordinary from the superordinary, the potentially evil from the possibly authentic.

Equally elucidative has been the explication of St. John of the Cross. In *Ascent of Mount Carmel*, he describes the devil's locutions as reflecting the desire of man, flowing from pride. Clearly, one must exercise caution in reacting and look for proper interpretation through prayer, holy people, and tangible fact.

Fortunately, I have not experienced the dark locutions of which St. Teresa writes. I assume that this is because my soul, young in conversion, is still wandering through the earlier "mansions" whereas St. Teresa had reached the innermost sanctum. Perhaps, too, the uncertainty that leads me to seek examination by those in spiritual authority has protected me. "I consider it quite certain," wrote St. Teresa, "that the devil will not deceive—and that God will not permit him to deceive—a soul which has no trust whatever in itself and is strengthened in faith."

Call Your Mother

In the early days after my conversion, prayer was a dialogue with the Voice. I would ask for lessons, and things would happen. Or, out of the blue, the Voice would task me with something that I did not want to do.

One example was the day when I was praying about something entirely different while walking around the grounds of Old Mission and the Voice interrupted me with the words, "Call your mother." To understand the significance of this, one must know that my mother (my only living parent) had continued to abuse my siblings and me even as adults and, when she was not under our direct observation, had abused our children. I had written her off. I had not been in touch with her for ten years, and I certainly had no intention of calling her for no reason. In fact, it would take some sleuthing to find out her phone number and where she lived.

I was sure I had misheard. "There is no way I am going to call my mother," I responded. "She is a bad person."

"She lives in grace," responded the Voice, and that was all.

I fumed and sputtered about it all being so unfair, arguing that she should not live in grace after everything she had done to her childen and grandchildren. I stomped about, punching the air in anger. I must have been an interesting sight to anyone walking by. Drunk or deranged?

The Voice would have its way, though. I finally realized that I had no right to judge Ma. (Oh, but how I wanted to!) Only God could do that, and if God said she lived in grace, who was I to say anything to the contrary?

That was then. Now I understand more. I understand, for example, that God is merciful while man is not, and we would like to recreate God in our own unmerciful image, with our marginal grasp on the balance scale of mercy and justice. After all, argues D. A. Carson (*How Long, O Lord? Reflections on Suffering and Evil*), if justice were enough, why did Jesus have to die?

Assuming that the Voice I had heard might be authentic, I figured I had better make a phone call. That was easier said than done. I tracked down my mother's phone number, yet I could not bring myself to make the call. Every time I felt the Presence around me, pushing me just a bit, I would resist. Finally, I turned to God and protested, "I cannot make this call. What can I say after ten years?"

The Voice immediately responded with one word: "Listen."

Sure, of course, I could just listen. And that is what I did. I called her. There was complete shock in her voice as she said, "Is this Beth? It sounds like Beth used to sound." I confirmed her guess, and she took over, talking non-stop for an hour, occasionally asking a question, filling me in on her life, telling me about her concerns. Clearly, she had mellowed as she approached her 80th year.

For a long time, I puzzled over the comment that Ma, after all she had done, lived in grace. Then, one day, in reading St. Paul, I came across the statement that God shines on both the just and the unjust. Of course! How else would any of us be forgiven?

In *When God Whispers Your Name*, Max Lucado addresses this issue of God's offering of grace to absolutely everyone. "I challenge you to find one soul who came to God seeking grace and did not receive it . . . one unlikely soul after another," he writes. "Seems...that God gives a lot more grace than we'd ever imagine. We could do the same." Well, it would be a while before I could do the same, but in time, with God's support, I could.

Forbidden Prayer

In the early days after my conversion, I received what seemed to me at the time to be a very strange locution about an individual from my previous job. At that point, I had spent two years working as the chief academic officer of a Middle Eastern university. Although I enjoyed the people part of the job, there were complications in meeting accreditation requirements, one of my most important responsibilities. Often, a decision I had to make for accreditation reasons was not palatable to Abdullah bin Mahmoud, the Middle Eastern billionaire who owned half the university. His primary goal was to make money, regardless of whom might suffer. So, while he and I enjoyed an unusually cordial relationship, given the acerbic relationship he has had with my predecessors and successors, there were times that I needed to use all my wiles to placate him. Sometimes I had to hold him back from firing a valuable employee for a minor, unintended offense or from verbally ripping into staff who were trying their best to their jobs. Other times, I had to push him forward—to pay people what they had earned or reimburse what they had spent. The tug-of-war over these issues never ended from the day I arrived until the day I left.

Self-love and profit permeated everything he did eleven months of the year. During Ramadan, however, he splashed money onto the community, feeding the poor in large numbers and making a flashy public show of charity in the name of the university. He himself spent Ramadan on *omra*, a voluntary pilgrimage, before Eid Al-Fitr (the short holiday right after Ramadan). In addition every year he made *hajj*, the pilgrimage to Mecca that all Muslims must make at least once in a lifetime before Eid al-Adha (the week-long holiday a couple months after Ramadan), seeming to understand this act in a way similar to which some young Catholic children misunderstand confession: confession sets you free to sin again, enjoying a clean record against which to work until the next confession comes along to clean up your new dirtiness. In this way, it seemed, Abdullah believed that he could "buy" salvation by once a year spending some of the money on the poor that he took from them during the rest of the year and making a pilgrimage to clean up his "dirt."

When Eid al-Fitr approached at the end of Ramadan, he would appear in town to celebrate in great joy. There were smiles all around, parties the likes of which none of us worker bees would likely see in any other context, and gifts for many. The same was true for Eid al-Adha. My first Eid al-Adha corresponded with my birthday, and Abdullah handed over the keys to a car, his birthday/Eid gift to me, at a birthday bash with 75 guests at one of the most lavish restaurants in town.

That was the dual nature of Abdullah. One never knew which side he would show. I fared well. I always had his smiles, and when he was about to attack an employee, I was always able to elicit his smiles again, not just for me but, more important, for those he might otherwise have harmed.

When I left the university, Abdullah owed me $30,000 I had advanced to the university bookstore to purchase books for the previous semester. He still does. At one point, I wrote to him, suggesting that if he had any conscience at all, that if the purification of his soul that was supposed to take place during *omra* and *hajj* really did occur, he could donate the amount he owed me, in his own name if he preferred, to the Middle East Institute of Special Education, which, as a new and struggling institute, could really use the money. He never did.

And so, one evening, a year later, I found myself walking around the grounds of Old Mission, as I did so frequently in the early days after my conversion and thinking about Abdullah for no particular reason other than that he came to mind. He had been a significant figure in my life in the most recent two-year period, so, not surprisingly, I thought about him on more than one occasion. I prayed for him, as well. After all, it seemed to me that he needed prayer in order to move from a rules-based religion and an impersonal God to a love-based spirituality and an immanent God. I wanted him to be able to feel the kinds of love, acceptance, and forgiveness I had felt. How different his life could be!

That particular evening, I was getting ready to wax persuasive about Abdullah when I was startled by the words, "Do not pray for him."

This made no sense to me. However, I felt I could not continue to pray for someone for whom I had been commanded not to pray. But was it God's voice? The command seemed out of line with something that God would ask me to do.

At the time, I accepted that it was okay if God chose not to provide greater clarity to me. Nonetheless, I have a difficult-to-repress, almost seething, desire to determine authenticity. In this case, as in other cases where I just do not know, I balanced benefit against harm, good against evil, and scripture against non-scripture and could not find a good reason not to follow these instructions. So, I ceased that particular prayer although I did not understand why I should.

I told the story to a friend who is a Protestant minister. She told me not to worry about authenticity and simply stop praying for him. She would do that for me. I hoped that was okay. I assume if it were not, she would find out in time.

Three years later I came across evidence that God sometimes does forbid us to pray for others. During a Bible Study class, I ran across verses in *Jeremiah* (*Jeremiah* 7:16, 11:14, and 14:11) in which God forbids Jeremiah to pray for the Israelites: "Pray no more for these people, Jeremiah. Do not weep or pray for them, and don't beg me to help them, for I will not listen to you."

When I read about the behavior of Jeremiah's people, I saw that Abdullah's behavior reflected a modern-day version of theirs. They would worship Baal and commit all manner of sins; then they would appear in the temple, expecting God's forgiveness and grace, after which they would return to sinning.

In *Amos* 4, I also found a potential explanation. The Israelites were more interested in a show of godliness than in being godly. They would go to church and assumed that they were protected by God after that and could sin as they wished. Their sacrifices were given for show. Like Abdullah, they were worldly wealthy but spiritually impoverished.

I am extremely grateful to God for putting closure to this incident. Knowing now what I did not know when I chose nonetheless to obey God has reinforced my willingness to obey with greater alacrity and confidence now. I am very glad I obeyed then and did not demand an explanation.

Confession

After my first confession, I was frustrated. (I now know that frustration does not come from God and freely admit that I had no right to be frustrated back then.) During a large-group, pre-Easter opportunity, set up in the church, not in the chapel where confessions are usually heard, I approached a priest I did not know. He turned out be a partially deaf Spaniard with limited English. I probably could have managed communicating with him in Spanish, but with his impaired hearing and my non-native accent, he would never have understood me. Not that he understood me in English! So, he gave me ten Our Fathers for a penance, not having understood or heard much of what I said.

Obviously, frustration did not put me in the right frame of mind for any penance to be sincere, but I made the attempt. Partway through the second iteration of Our Father, I felt myself being pulled by the elbow to the outside of the church. Once outside, I complained to God, "He didn't listen. I could have said that I burned down the town and murdered ten priests, and he would have given me the same penance!"

"*I* listen," answered the Voice.

Since then, I have come to understand better the nature of confession, as well as the role of the priest. Having been "instructed" by the Voice, though, I came to that understanding much more quickly than I might have otherwise.

Come Closer

During Mass, I sit in the last section of pews, sometimes in the very last pew. Contrary to what one might think, I am not far from God there. In fact, I find God's presence to be very strong inside Old Mission Church, so strong that when I approach the altar, I involuntarily tremble. Deep within me, simultaneously all around me, and spread throughout the church but epicentered at the altar is a power so immense that it exceeds my ability to comprehend. In the back of the church, I am free to bask quietly in the radiant presence of God's love.

There is a part of me that feels unworthy, having spent so many decades as an atheist, to approach the altar, that awesome place of divine glory, and so I sit in the remoter pews. When I look around, I see people who have spent their entire lives worshiping God, and then I begin to feel like an interloper even though I know that God wants me there. Especially difficult for me were daily Masses the winter before last when the only warm place in our unheated church during an unusually cold spell was around the altar, where chairs were placed for the few of us who attended daily

Mass. I would shake throughout the entire Mass. It was not from the cold but from the overwhelming sense of God's powerful presence.

There was a time, however, when I was impelled to approach this glorious Presence. Nurse J, who had come to visit me, preferred to sit in the front section of pews. I described to her my reaction whenever I came close to the altar, so we compromised on the last row of the front section. She was a cradle Catholic who knows much more than I do about God and God's church. Most of *my* "knowing" comes from experiencing God directly although I do read voraciously. *Her* knowing came from catechism lessons and a lifetime of church activity. She was, however, to have an experience similar to mine.

As she was getting on the plane to return home, she heard a very clear voice say, "Tell Beth to come closer." She immediately knew that this referred to my reluctance to approach the altar. Surprisingly, she never questioned what she had heard. As soon as she arrived home, she called and told me.

"I don't know if I can do that, Nurse J," I told her. "I am afraid."

"Well, I think you better at least try," she responded. I knew she was right, but I was really nervous about it. I also knew that if I shared this nervousness with anyone else in the congregation, they would consider me odd. And if I told them what Nurse J had heard, they would likely consider both of us delusional. So, I said nothing, but I knew I would obey. Since my conversion, I always obey, which is quite strange, considering that I had previously always been considered a rebel.

At vespers the following Saturday after receiving the host, I paused nervously at the altar railing, silently stating, "Okay, Lord, here I am; I came all the way to the front and instead of quickly passing on to the cup and returning to the last pew, I am still here."

"Not enough; come alone" was the response. Alone? Alone was even more frightening! Alone, in fact, was highly frightening! But alone it would be.

Old Mission is considered a tourist attraction. Therefore, it is open all day every day. Nonetheless, there are times that it is empty, and I know when those times are. So, I came back—alone, as ordered.

As I knelt at the altar railing, I saw what looked like heat waves rising from the altar. As I watched, the height of the waves grew higher and higher. Concerned that my eyes were playing tricks on me, I pulled my driving glasses out of my purse and donned them. Once again, the waves started as a thin layer on top of the altar and grew higher and higher. And then I heard the words: "Do not be afraid to come all the way to Me."

I do not know how long I knelt there. I could not immediately move. I did not want to move. I am still sorting out what this experience means and why God graced me with it. Maybe I will never know. Maybe it is not meant for me to know. If I am supposed to know, God will send someone or another experience to teach me.

Write for Me

The next time, the Voice came with imagery and a tall order. As I was driving to work one morning, I was startled (I don't think I will ever not be startled) by the Voice saying to me, "I gave you the gift of words. Use them for me, and on the basis of what you write, speak."

Now here was something I was certain I was not qualified to do. I argued, "I don't write those kinds of books. I write professional books for specialists in my field. I would not know how to write something about You or for You." Why God puts up with my argumentativeness and does not simply wipe me out with the swat of a thought or give up on me, I do not know.

The response to my argument was immediate. Against the clouds, I saw a pink-covered book with a moving black pen. "I will guide your pen," came the response.

That presented me with a dilemma. First, what on earth was I supposed to write? There was not much direction in what I had heard. Second, when on earth was I supposed to do it? My job required 60-70 hours a week. Third, by the time I got to work I was wondering if I had really heard what I remembered hearing.

Although I wanted to, I could not ignore the vision and Voice. The Voice, as it always does, had seared itself into my memory. I fussed about it for four months, trying to figure out what to do about the tasking and wondering if it were authentic. At the time, I knew absolutely nothing about such things as locutions. I had not yet heard about St. Teresa of Avila. I knew nothing about the Desert Fathers. I had not yet read the contemporary interpretation of St. Teresa's experiences with locutions in the works of Fr. Thomas Dubay, who believed that the experiences of the Desert Fathers and the Carmelites of St. Teresa's era are experienced by people today and whose book, *Authenticity*, has become my constant companion. Unnerved and lost, I knew I should do something, yet at the same time, I did not think I had the skills for it. Moreover, my reasonable, rational mind wanted to dismiss the locution and vision as hallucination. However, something would not let me ignore the tasking. So, I turned to a priest for help. The priest thought that the tasking might be genuine and suggested that I follow through and see what happened.

In following through, I often asked for help and received it. On one occasion, when I asked, the book title popped into my head: *Blest Atheist*. This title, ironically, has landed the book in the hands of atheists looking for something quite different, but perhaps that was not unintentional. Oddly enough, too, the book cover turned out to be pink.

After publication of the book, *Blest Atheist* became a blog (re-established as 100th Lamb when the Blest Atheist blog was hijacked). That blog led to other blogs. Perhaps blogging is more important than the book itself. Nonetheless, my next book, *Raising God's Rainbow Makers*, is underway—if I can stop blogging long enough to finish it.

These days I try to use my words for God because I know that any talent with words that I might have comes from God. Therefore, my words belong to God. Not only am I writing, but the rest of the message—"on the basis of what you write, speak"—has started to occur with any effort on my part. I have been asked to speak at organizations, at chapel sessions, and to other groups. And, surprisingly to my family and friends, I have become a catechist where I use my words every other week with teenagers.

A Sign, Please

Not long after I started to receive verbal taskings, I began to have some doubts, mostly put into my head when others started questioning me about these experiences. In the early days after my conversion, I shared these experiences openly, thinking that all believers have them.

One of the people who questioned what I was telling him suggested that I ask for a sign that the Voice was indeed divine. About the same time, the Voice had become quieter in speaking to me, ebbing into more of a whisper then a voice. So, the next time I heard it, I said, "I cannot hear You," and the message was repeated more audibly (to my ear, anyway).

"How do I know this is You?" I asked. "Please give me a sign that it is Your voice that I am hearing."

"I will not give you a sign," the Voice responded. "Trust that it is My voice the way you trusted me to heal your colleague."

Had I been familiar with the *Bible* at the time, I might not have been surprised by this pronouncement. When the scribes and Pharisees asked for a sign, Jesus told them that he would give them no sign, saying, "An evil and adulterous generation seeks after a sign, and no sign will be given to it except the sign of the prophet Jonah [the resurrection] (*Matthew* 12:39). Thomas, after the resurrection, is told by Jesus in *John* 20:29 that we are to believe without seeking proof: "Because you have seen me, you have believed; blessed are those who have not seen, yet have believed."

So, I was left with the plea yearned in *Psalm 119*: "Give me discernment, Lord." Only sometimes is that plea answered. When it is not, I wait. I have found that one comes to know God better in the waiting than in the doing or the knowing.

About this same time, I learned that not all believers interact with God in this way. In fact, most tell me that they have never heard this Voice. Truly, I do not understand why God chooses to interact with various people differently. I can suppose that it is because we are all different one from another, but only God really knows why. As Jean-Pierre Caussade wrote in *Abandonment to Divine Providence*, "Perfection consists in doing the will of God, not in understanding His designs." Likewise, St. John of the Cross (*Ascent of Mount Carmel*) suggests that "God grants these favours to whom He wills and for what reason He wills. For it may come to pass that a person will have performed many good works, yet He will not give him these touches of His favour; and another will have done far fewer good works, yet He will give him them to a most sublime degree and in great abundance." With growing faith, I have given up my intense need to understand. I simply obey. In doing that, I have achieved peace.

Authenticity

I any reticent about sharing my experiences of what I call "the Voice" with people in my community, given the negative reactions I often receive. Among the most vociferous of those reactions came from Fr. Dan.

Fr. Dan was leading a retreat on the topic of Franciscan spirituality, a popular topic in my part of the world, where the missions were established by the Franciscans. At the very first session, Fr. Dan presented a part of St. Francis's biography. In doing so, he interpreted it somewhat differently from what I was used to and made a pronouncement that floored me and caused me to talk to him separately.

"We should be careful in how we interpret historical information," he said. "St. Francis did not hear a real voice telling him to rebuild God's church. Rather, it was something that he thought should be done, and so he 'heard' in his mind the words that led to his rebuilding not only San Damiano but the more abstract 'church.'"

What? St. Francis was confused as to whether he heard, sensed, or thought something? Convinced that if St. Francis said he *heard* a voice he really did *hear* a voice and bolstered by my own experiences and my readings of the experiences of St. Teresa of Avila, I approached Fr. Dan during the break and asked him whether he thought that God ever speaks to people in a voice.

"No," he responded. "That's not the way God works."

"But what about all those times in the Bible when someone heard the voice of God? Was it only in their minds, too?"

"Yes," he said.

"Don't you think that God can choose to speak in a way that people hear?"

"No," he said curtly.

After that, I retreated even more deeply into non-disclosure of my experiences except with my prayer group and on my one blog that is dedicated to the topic of modern mysticism. The response of blog readers gave me courage to continue sharing, and the fact that I was not alone among those in the blogosphere also gave me courage. Learning that others have parallel experiences, finding some historical descriptions of similar experiences, and, most important, realizing that I have no say in how God communicates has helped me overcome my reluctance to put these experiences into writing. The fact that I do not know why God chooses one means of communication for me and other means for others no longer troubles me. It could be as simple as my being too "dense" to understand anything more subtle, or it could be, as someone suggested (I don't reall who), that God has not stopped talking to people but people have stopped listening. I am simply happy that God is *willing* to communicate with me.

The best elucidation I have been able to find lies in the differentiation between the New Age Movement, Christianity, and Phariseeism suggested by Mark and Patti Virkler (*Am I Being Deceived?*). Modern-day Pharisees, in the Virklers' delineation, do not believe that visions are for today, do not look for them, and usually see negative images if they see anything at all. Proponents of the New Age Movement believe that visions come from the spiritual world at large, look for visions, and believe that they can center themselves to receive them. Christians, the third group, believe that visions come from God, accept visions as a gift, and act in faith upon them. One could extend this delineation as well to locutions although the Virklers do not. That thought has helped me balance the negative reaction of Fr. Dan with my own experiences—that and the comment by a priest whom I completely trust that he disagrees with Fr. Dan.

The Virklers go on to aver that New Agers do receive clear messages from the spirit world. However, because they are not receiving messages exclusively from God but rather "are receiving messages from many spirits, including evil spirits and perhaps even Satan," the message, its clarity aside, "will be defiled" because the source is at best unclear and at worst itself defiled.

Because of the similarity between the Christian and New Age experiences, the question of authenticity of the messages and tasks I received continued to trouble me until I came across Fr. Thomas Dubay's inordinately helpful book, *Authenticity*. It was the fourth or fifth of Fr. Thomas's books I had read. All of the books were helpful to me, but this one especially reached me where I needed instruction, understanding, support, and advice. I wrote to Fr. Thomas to tell him how helpful I had found that book. I told him of some of my experiences, of the details of my quest to determine their authenticity, and of my questions and concerns. I did not ask for a response and did not expect one. Nonetheless, a few weeks later, I received handwritten comments on my letter from Fr. Thomas, who apologized for the format, saying that he had just arrived home from a trip very fatigued but wanted nonetheless to respond to my note immediately. He told me that he thought that my experiences, as described, were likely authentic. He explained why, commented on my comments, and suggested some answers to my questions. His letter gave me greater confidence in moving more deeply into contemplation and not pulling away from God at the most intimate moments.

Even though God earlier refused to give me a sign and asked me to trust that what I was hearing was indeed God's voice, it seems that God had relented after all and sent me a sign through Fr. Thomas, first via the book and then more personally and directly by Fr. Thomas's hand. I will always seek to confirm authenticity from a knowledgeable priest or from objective events; that is Fr. Thomas's guidance in *Authenticity*. It is good guidance because it would be easy, I think, to misinterpret, to think I hear what I would merely like to hear and not what God is saying.

Fr. Thomas passed away soon afterward, and his passing feels like a personal loss. I now treasure those handwritten notes. I like to think that before Fr. Thomas joined the communion of saints, one of his smaller acts was to serve as the conduit between God and me in the matter of authenticity.

Tasks

Shura could be considered one of the first tasks that God assigned to me although I was completely unaware of the tasking. After all, at that time, I was still a believer in waiting.

Tasks have come in a variety of guises. In some things, I get clarity; in others, I remain confused through to the end. In yet others, I am never sure if I *have* reached the end.

When matters are very unclear, following the advice of Fr. Thomas Dubay, I either wait or seek out a priest for interpretation. In some cases, I can use the tests proposed by St. Teresa of Avila, and they work for me:

(1) Is the locution (or task) anti-Scriptural?

(2) Is it somehow coming from my own subconscious, i.e. something that I personally would want to do, or could it be simply internal monologue?

(3) Did the locution or vision come as a response to some request, or did it appear spontaneously and unexpectedly?

(4) Are the locutions long and rambling or are they succinct and searing?

In the case of the tasks described in this chapter, each time I could say:

(1) The tasks have not been in any way opposed to Scripture. That would scare me! I would wonder where the manifestations were coming from!

(2) The tasks could not have been anything I might have imagined because most of them I do not want to do—they are things I do not know how to do, take time I don't think I have, or put me in embarrassing positions. Who would want any of that?

(3) The manifestations always take me by surprise and usually shock me because they intrude into something else I am doing at the moment. For whatever reason, they don't come while I am sleeping or daydreaming. Instead, they intrude sharply while I am involved in something unrelated: driving, walking, reading.

(4) The locutions are always brief, sometimes confusingly so. It would be much easier to decipher a long, rambling message for English rhetoric ensures redundancy in most rambles. In fact, redundancy is a key to comprehension in most linguistic systems. So, a message that is so brief as to be stripped of any redundancy, as has been every locution I have received, can leave meaning ambiguous. The succinct nature of these locutions, though, sears them into my memory; I cannot forget one word.

Steve Schultz in *Can't You Speaker Louder, God?* contends that while God speaks to most people in a still voice that is hard to discern and sounds like one's own voice, which can create confusion with our own actual voice (i.e. our own desires or thoughts), God speaks audibly to a few individuals, not necessarily chosen for their worthiness but for reasons that we may never know. I suspect that in my case it is a matter of being oblivious to the world around me, let alone the world inside me, and it takes a series of conks on the head, so to speak, to get my attention. Once I am standing at attention, however, and am certain of authenticity, I spare no effort in accomplishing divinely imposed tasks.

While there is something recognizable about the Voice (as Jesus said, the sheep recognize the Shepherd's voice), I take the locutions to someone spiritually knowledgeable, given the possibility of deception and/or self-deception. (How many times has a despiccable action been taken, using the words, "God told me to...," simply because on a subcnscious level someone *wanted* to do something?). Where I can reach a reasonable conclusion of authenticity, I do as asked, regardless of desire or consequence. After all, when you love someone deeply, you do not want to disappoint; that's the way it is for me with God and these tasks. The remainder I hold in abeyance until such time as God makes clear the expectations of me.

The Children of Palomar

The first time I attended the Spanish Mass at Old Mission, a young priest from Colombia was celebrating the Mass. Charming, dedicated, spiritual, and drawn to people, he found many people drawn to him. His name was Padre Julio (Fr. Julio).

More than building a congregation, which he seemed to do effortlessly, Padre Julio had a very special goal: to improve the lives and career options of the children of his home area of Palomar where youngsters were being pulled into violence by insurgents because they had few alternatives. He wanted Americans to experience the blessing of helping him help the children, and many did, becoming sponsors for a host of children in the surrounding towns. He planned to build a school on a self-sustaining farm. He had a start: two tractors donated by the local rotary club.

No voice told me to help Padre, but somehow I understood that I was supposed to help him. I offered to help, but we had a problem. He avoided English speakers because he could not speak English. My spoken Spanish is weak, but I can understand. So, we began a written correspondence, and after a while, he gathered the courage to talk to me, with him speaking Spanish and me speaking English.

At the time, he had someone working on a Spanish-language website, but he was paying a high fee for a designer with limited skills. That person had taken his money and not delivered. Padre Julio did not know how to deal with him, so he turned the problem over to me. I forced the designer to finish the website, but it looked unprofessional. So, I gathered my family together, along with a friend from Colombia who is a professional translator. I translated the Spanish website documents into English, and then I wrote a website around them in English. My friend translated the English site, including localizing the codes, into Spanish. Donnie designed the website and created the graphics. Our son, Shane, who studied programming, wrote the html. Our "son," Blaine, whom we took into our home from the local barrio when he was abandoned by his mother at age 13, was working in Illinois as a commercial web designer. He flew home to provide the finishing flourishes. We had a website! It brought in money and let people follow the progress of Padre's projects. It also shared letters from the children and encouraged more people to become sponsors.

About the time that we finished the website, I left for Bahrain where I had been asked to help with some projects for the Ministry of Education. Arabs being very hospitable people, they would not allow me to pay for my first meal there, even though the ministry was providing me *per diem*. The same thing happened with the second meal. At that point, during prayer the idea came into my head that I could give my unused *per diem* to Padre Julio for the children of Palomar. I wrote to him, telling him that I had promised God to pass along any unused *per diem*. Surprisingly, or perhaps not so, I did not pay for even one meal while there. When I returned, I handed Padre Julio a check for $1000 for his children.

Over time, Padre Julio became a good friend, offering Mass for our family's difficult moments, such as our daughter Noelle's emergency brain surgery, Shane's emergency appendectomy and internal body wash, and Shane's unflappable daughter Nikolina being born with OEIS Complex, a condition in which not all organs are present, adequately formed, or appropriately located. In return, I taught Padre Julio English when the bishop assigned him to celebrate English Masses. Our textbooks were the English *Bible* and *Santa Biblia* along with audio files from online English homilies and *La Vida y Fey (Life and Faith)*. Padre Julio may have learned English from me, but I learned a lot about faith from him. It seems that God had found a way to teach me faster than I was learning through my own means!

In 2009, Padre Julio returned to Colombia. Using funds collected to date, he began the initial implementation of his dream, sending back letters from the children and pictures of the project.

Today, Padre Julio is assigned as pastor at a parish in California. The farm and school have been built and are operating. We still see Padre Julio. Occasionally, he comes to Salts to meet with his foundation and invites Donnie and me to a private Mass, celebrated in the president's home. Once we visited him at his parish eight hours away. Recently, when we bought a new house, he came to San Ignatio from San Diego, picking up his brother, Padre Mario, a visiting priest in a nearby town. Together with our friends, Padre Julio and Padre Mario blessed our new home in their own special way in Spanish and English.

Helping Padre was not a task from God. It is an ever-growing gift from God.

God's Impeccable Timing

I had taken the day off from work, but that does not mean that the day was quiet. In the middle of running around on errands, I attempted to add a modicum of quiet to my day by taking time out to attend noon Mass in San Ignatio.

Our parish priest was out of town, so Fr. K, who is assigned to another parish, came to celebrate Mass. When Fr. K, who had had trouble finding our chapel, came into Mass, he seemed to be out of breath from hurrying. No one paid much attention to that until toward the end of Mass when he stated that he did not feel well. He then sat down and remained quiet.

After a few minutes, he finished Mass, apologized, and disappeared into the sacristy. An out-of-towner who had attended Mass with a group of school children visiting the mission followed him in. It fortuitously turned out that this visitor was an EMT. He was concerned, but when Fr. K insisted he was okay, he emerged from the sacristy, saying that Fr. K did not want help. He left.

Theresa, a parishioner, was right behind the EMT visitor, and I was right behind her. Two mothers are more difficult to push away than an EMT. Theresa offered to take Fr. K to the hospital, 17 miles away. He declined her offer, saying that he felt okay, that it was just a pinched nerve or something that was causing the left side of his body to be temporarily paralyzed. (That is "feeling okay?")

No, this was *not* okay. The EMT felt that Fr. K needed a doctor. Thank God, he had been there because otherwise Theresa and I might have been misled into thinking that Fr. K did not need our help. I offered to take Fr. K's car back to his parish if he would let Theresa take him to the hospital. He said that he did not want to be a bother. Well, mothers don't listen to that kind of dissembling answer. They have heard it many times before from their little boys (and big boys).

"That's why you have a parish," I objected. "Parishioners are here to help you."

After all, God gives us priests for our needs. In return, God gives us to the priests. It is not a dependent relationship; it is a symbiotic relationship. We belong to each other.

Fr. K hesitated, and I knew I had him. I held out my hand for his keys. He dutifully handed them over to me, explained what his handicapped-enabled car looked like and how to work it. I left to go home to get Donnie, so that he could drive Fr. K's car and I could follow in our car so that we had a way home. We easily found the parochial school parking space where Fr. K asked us to leave his car.

When Donnie and I got back to the mission after our half-hour round trip, the ambulance had arrived for Fr. K. He had had another episode. As it turned out, he needed immediate surgery.

I shudder to think what would have happened if he had driven back on his own. Thank God, I was off work and was there to help. (Oh, that was probably God's plan all along!)

Bring Him to Me

Months passed before I heard the Voice again. When I did, I was startled both by the hearing of it and by the content.

I had again been doing some consultation for the Ministry of Education in Bahrain. That particular day I had finished early and was reading in my hotel room. The sun does not set until quite late during the hot days of early fall in Manama, and at 4:00 in the afternoon, the sun was streaming toward the Bahrain desert at full throttle, providing me with a flood of natural light for enjoying the book I had brought with me.

As I was reading, seated at the window, four distinct words pulled me instantly from my book and chair: "Bring him to Me."

Simultaneously, I saw the image of Aymon, an employee who worked for me. Or, more accurately, who worked for a supervisor three rungs in the ladder below me. I, however, did know Aymon and knew that he was a devout Catholic.

"He *is* with you," I responded instinctively. My talking-back trait that drove my mother to fury has not changed.

From God, there was no fury. All I got was a short comment: "Not enough."

Oh, my! This tasking was going to be complicated and one whose authenticity, given the immediateness of the assignment and my location, I had to assume simply from the familiar sound of the Voice.

How on earth was I going to approach Aymon? Write to him and tell him what I had been told? He would think I was bonkers! Nonetheless, I clearly had to "bring him" to God even though I knew (thought) that he was devout. I took a deep breath, turned on my computer, hooked up to the Internet, and sent a brief note of query: "Is everything all right with you?"

Days and nights occurring at different times in the Middle East and the USA, it was the next day before I got his response. Indeed, he said, everything was not only all right but also going swimmingly well. He went on to talk about his children's recent accomplishments at school, his success at work, and even his wife's success at her job. He was not making this easy for me at all. Feeling considerably foolish but nonetheless mission-impelled, I typed back five words: "I mean with your soul." What a strange thing to write to an employee!

I waited impatiently for the next day to arrive, wondering how he would interpret this highly personal intrusion into his life. My note was not a typical topic of discussion between people so far apart in a hierarchy. On the other hand, I have tried diligently and successfully to flatten our hierarchy.

When the answer came, it was perplexingly ambiguous. Had it been a conversation, I would have labeled his response dissembling. Since it was written, I can only say that Aymon did not answer the question directly. Rather, he made unclear references to future concerns in what seemed to me to be gibberish.

I did not have to wait long, however, for a fuller understanding. In the middle of the next night, I received an urgent phone call from Aymon's supervisor. The husband of another employee, a Muslim, had called the supervisor and threatened to sue our organization because his wife was having an affair with Aymon. Now the "bring him to Me" made a lot of sense!

I explained to the supervisor that he did not need to worry about the angry husband. The husband could not sue the organization. We had not required his wife to have an affair with a co-worker, nor had anything taken place at work. We talked a bit about why the husband would feel like he should contact the supervisor, the differences between Muslim and non-Muslim marriages, and the marital fidelity that is required especially on the part of the wife by Sharia law. Not without reason, I was a bit concerned for the female employee. Fortunately, others in her community had already stepped up to protect her.

The first-line supervisor was calmed. After sending me additional information by email and being fully reassured, again, by me that there was nothing to worry about, he was able to go on with business as usual. I, however, could not. I still had not completed the task of "bring him to Me."

There being nothing more that I could do from a distance, I filed away all the e-notes just in case I were to need them (now evidence of the remarkableness of what had transpired). A few days later, I completed my consult in Bahrain and returned home.

As soon as I arrived back in California, I called the employee into my office at the end of the day for what turned out to be a two-hour conversation. While his having an affair was really none of my business, it clearly had been made my business. I told Aymon I knew about the affair and asked why he had told me that all was well with his soul when this was going on. He said nothing. Then I told him about the Voice and being told "bring him to Me." At that point, Aymon broke down, stuttering that he knew he had a great wife and felt remorseful. I suggested that he tell her before someone else did. He demurred. I asked him to consider this strongly and to get guidance from his priest.

"Oh, no," he said. "There is no way I am going to confess this to my priest; he knows my whole family." Well, he should have thought about that ahead of time.

He begged me to find someone who did not know him. I refused, insisting that his own priest was the appropriate person, certain that in his current state he would be less than candid with anyone else, and pointing out that he was not confessing to the priest but to God. I did, however, take him to Old Mission to pray together.

We had a second meeting a short while after our late-evening prayer on the mission grounds. Aymon told me that he had talked to his wife, realizing that I was right. She had forgiven him. He also had been able to put aside his pride, go to confession, and achieve reconciliation with the help of his own priest.

So, all is well, I guess, that ends well. I tried the best I knew how, not having been given any further instructions or any explicit guidance, to accomplish the "bring him to Me" task by sending Aymon to somone else. Was that what God had wanted? Only God only knows!

Of course, the age-old question nagged: why me? God only knows! Yeah, that would be right. God does know. I don't, and I suppose I don't need to know.

I am getting much better these days at accepting the not knowing of it all. Not knowing why people and things get put in my path. Not knowing what exactly is expected of me. Not knowing if how I respond meets with God's approval. None of that matters much to me any more. I know that God loves me. I know that I honestly try to do as I am asked. If I need to know more than that, I will be given to know it. If I need to do more, I will be tasked with doing more. In the interim, I am happy to serve God in whatever way I can, even if imperfectly. As Anne Rice (*Called Out of Darkness: A Spiritual Confession*) wrote of her own conversion, "in seeking to know everything, I'd been, all of my life, missing the entire point."

Adrian

Months had passed after hearing the Voice in Bahrain. God must be on silent running, I thought, when, unexpectedly as usual, another task popped up: Adrian. At the time, I was volunteering at San Ignatio Shelter and Soup, often called Triple S. Run by a Christian foundation, Triple S provided beds and blankets to the homeless in San Ignatio and fed them three simple meals each day.

Not long after I began volunteering at Triple S, Adrian became my shift leader. I welcomed Adrian, hoping to learn from him. We held, by organizational policy, informal semi-monthly meetings to discuss how we provided our services, determine what was needed, account for donations, and learn how others ran similar programs. I had always enjoyed these meetings, especially because they had also been opportunities for faith sharing.

Soon after he became shift leader, Adrian moved our meetings from the Triple S conference room to his spacious shift-leader's office, of which he was button-busting proud, and I wondered if, in part, he wanted to show it off. Once inside, though, he oddly ushered us to a small table in the dimly lit, windowless, oppressive anteroom. There, meetings became passive sessions where Adrian berated and belittled us for various perceived infractions of Foundation rules. If issues of substance arose, he immediately and self-importantly changed the topic back to rules and regulations.

Taking on Adrian

Adrian is soft-spoken and protrays himself as a good listener. In reality, he listens but does not hear. His cognitive deafness troubled me less than his eyes. Whenever one of us would bring up a spiritual topic, he would look at that person with vacant eyes. Initially, I paid scant attention. After all, Adrian was senior to me and the religious education director in his own parish.

After a few meetings, though, we volunteers compared notes. All of us had been perturbed by the same aspects of our meetings: vacuous prayer, a feeling of uneasiness in the windowless room and with the aimless conversations that took place there, and a perception of being treated with condescension. Adrian, who lived in the upper-class suburb of a near-by city, did not like poor people, an arrogance that extended to our entire shift since we all came from a small and financially struggling Mexican-American town. In addition to volunteering at Triple S, many of our shift volunteers routinely emptied all the change from their shallow pockets into the coffers of the church or handed out their last dollar to someone on a street corner. None of this mattered to Adrian. He perhaps did not consider that the poor are also made in the image of God and that "whoever mocks the poor has contempt for their maker" (*Proverbs* 17:5). In fact, he seemed to despise the kinds of generosity that the spirituality of a mission town brings. We wondered why he would volunteer with Triple S and figured that perhaps being a shift leader satisfied an ego need since he held no community-valued position in his everyday job as a local IRS auditor. From deep inside him oozed hubris and ambition. (One is reminded of the secular ambition that confused St. Augustine, as he related in his *Confessions*, and kept him from God for many years.) Adrian's complacent attitude, vacant eyes, and vacuous smile reminded me of the insensitive nurse in the movie, *One Flew over the Cuckoo's Nest*, or the "unreflective eyes" ascribed to fallen spirits.

Some of the volunteers began coming to me individually. Perhaps they sensed that as a manager in my professional life, I could provide some leadership skills they needed in dealing with Adrian. Perhaps it was divinely motivated. I don't know. Knowing is not important.

The first to come was Earnest. An emulatable example of humility, he scrambles to make a living. Taking time off from his regular job for our volunteer meetings, the length of which Adrian had doubled, meant more than four hours without pay each month. He accepted that sacrifice, but I felt it was unfair. His personal discomfort came from Adrian's flippant response to his spiritual comments.

The next meeting Earnest could not attend. Neither could several others, including Nancy. So, only Onyx and I attended. Before the meeting, Onyx, also openly disdained by Adrian, likely because Onyx is a recovering alcoholic and unemployed, begged me to bring up the length and content of the meetins with Adrian, as well as our discomfort in his dark anteroom.

Unsure of how best to approach the situation, I had called a friend, who led a different Triple S shift. He felt that I should raise the concerns to Adrian. He offered to approach Adrian on our behalf, and in hindsight, perhaps I should have opted for that approach. However, at the time, I felt that Onyx and I could reason with Adrian. So, near the end of the meeting, I brought up our concerns.

The response shocked me. Adrian insisted that his preferences as shift leader took precedence over our needs and concerns. He was the most important person in the group he repeatedly stated even though we were not challenging his importance. Then he suggested that if we did not like it, we could leave the Foundation until we were ready to do things his way.

A couple of days later, Nancy called me to find out what had happened at the meeting. Before I could tell her about the awkward discussion, she volunteered that she had not come with us because she was uneasy being in Adrian's anteroom. "Would you let your daughter go there?" she asked.

Practicing the presence of God in the vein of Brother Lawrence is something I do all the time. However, Nancy's question made me realize that I lost the sense of God's presence whenever I opened Adrian's door and regained it when I left. What I was feeling while there, what Nancy did not want to expose her daughter to seemed to be a sense of Evil. I thought about all of Adrian's religious activities. How can there be evil *inside* the church, I wondered at that time. Now I have seen that where Good treads, there also hovers Evil. One may not sense the conjoining of Good and Evil because Evil quietly awaits its opportunity. As St. Paul told the Ephesians, "We do not wrestle against flesh and blood, but against . . . the spiritual forces of evil in the heavenly places" (*Ephesians* 6:2).

I do not believe that Adrian is evil. Rather, his profound lack of humility may have allowed Evil to lead him where otherwise he might know better than to go. Certainly, it seemed that Adrian was controlled by Evil: his spookily soft monotone, his empty eyes, and his avoidance of spiritual discussions. Unnerved by the situation in which we found ourselves,we volunteers on Adrian's shift discussed whether to continue exposing ourselves to the unhealthy team meetings, where we seemed to be meeting Adrian on a battlefield of spiritual warfare.

An Image

Following this discussion with Nancy, I prayed for direction. The response, an image of Jesus overturning the tables in the temple, confused me. What was that supposed to mean? I prayed more. Every time I prayed, the same image appeared.

I left the question unresolved for several days, then once again turned to God for help. Again, that same image appeared. I did not know how to interpret it. I shared it with my Bible Studies leader, but he did not know how to interpret it, either.

From out of that image bubbled anger and a sense of needing to *do* something. After all, the image and story were of Jesus *doing* something. So, I contacted Adrian, reiterating the requests that had been made at the previous meeting. He responded by phoning all the others in a divide-and-conquer power play that only drove us to each other to cope with this attempted manipulation. I asked Adrian to talk to all of us as a group, but he demurred.

As a team, we decided to make a written request to meet with the Foundation Directors. Somehow, though, the chairman misplaced our letter, so there was no meeting. Some of us began looking into volunteering with a different organization.

Then, Nancy ran into one of the Board members, Laura, in a bookstore in another city. (None of us can convince ourselves that this meeting was coincidental.) Out tumbled Nancy's concerns, after which Laura told Nancy the history: Adrian had not been their choice to be shift leader but had appropriated the position for himself in a bullying manner that left the Board members without recourse. At least some of the Board members were as uncomfortable with Adrian as we were!

Laura asked Nancy to convince me to call her. I called, and we talked for more than an hour. Encouraged, I told Laura everything up to that point, including the image of Jesus overturning tables in the temple, sharing that I could not make sense of the image other than the feeling that I was supposed to *do* something related to it. Laura had an interesting interpretation: "I think it means that God does not like evil infiltrating His foundation." That was the first time that the word "evil" had been spoken. Before Laura hung up, I had promised to meet with the Board.

Long after the incident with Adrian had reached a zenith and subsided, someone pointed out to me that when Jesus called the temple a "den of thieves," he was referring to two things. First, selling animals for sacrifices was a desecration of the Lord's house. Second, the poor, loved by Jesus, were denigrated in the temple sales for they could not afford to buy the kinds of "nice" sacrifices that the wealthy could. The latter thought made sense when it came to the aptness of the image to Adrian.

Clarification

After I hung up with Laura, I complained to God: "Lord, You know that I am a verbal learner. I need words, not pictures, to understand. I will try to grow in the ways you seem to want me to, but in this case, I really need verbal input."

Then I drew bath water, the remaining ritual of the day. As the water filled the tub, I debated whether to take into the tub with me a book that I was partway through reading or the *Bible*.

"My Word." Out of nowhere came the Voice, startling me as usual.

So, the *Bible* it was. I haphazardly opened the *Bible* and found myself staring at a passage I had never read before: *Ezekiel* 30. As I read through the chapter, a lament for Egypt and God's threat of destruction, I saw many parallels to my own situation. Once again, a prayer had been answered. I had *words*, not an image—except, uh-oh, as I read, I became less certain of my interpretation. Here was a tale of arrogance punished. Certainly, Adrian's arrogance deserved to be punished, but the adjective used in the verse was "her," referring to a nation, Egypt. Now, Adrian was definitely a "he," and I am definitely a "she," but in most historical documents, nations are frequently referred to as "she." So, confusion appeared anew.

Once again, I cried out for help in exasperation at myself for not being able to understand what was apparently supposed to be obvious. "So, Lord, whom do You see as arrogant? Me or Adrian?"

The response was immediate and clear: "Let Adrian know he cannot treat *My* people this way." As with other locutions, every word is seared into my memory forever.

Now that I had what seemed to be clarity, I definitely had to let Adrian know. Whatever were to happen to me or my reputation (people tend to think you are nuts if you tell them that you experience locutions), I would carry out any tasking that so much effort had gone into making clear.

When I returned, Earnest, laboring under the assumption that I might stop volunteering at Triple S, asked to speak to me urgently. He told me that he had been praying about the situation and was certain that I was supposed to finish what I had started. For some reason, Earnest thought it meant I should stay long-term at Triple S, but I understood it to mean that I should see the tasking through to its finish: discuss Adrian's maltreatment of God's people with the Foundation directors.

The Meeting

The morning of the meeting with the directors, to which Nancy accompanied me, I was understandably nervous, knowing that I would have to talk about things mystical and not knowing whether the other directors would be as accepting of them as Laura had been. Nancy and I attended the same Mass that morning. There, the person leading the choir made a mistake and gave the wrong page number for the last hymn we were to sing. The song we ended up singing was "Be Not Afraid." The powerful images in that song brought a sense of strength, comfort, and, most important, confidence:

> *Be not afraid.*
> *I go with you always.*
> *Come, follow me.*
> *And I will give you rest.*

Nancy asked me after Mass if I had picked up on the mistake and its possible significance. Of course! I also was aware that in Biblical times God's appearance on the scene or a message or task sent from God was usually preceded by the words, "Be not afraid!" Obviously, I am not the only one to experience apprehension when greeted with divine intervention.

I found that once we were at the meeting, with Adrian present as well, I was not afraid. I did not feel alone. Of course, Nancy's support helped, as did the clear willingness of the other directors to listen to our concerns. Even more helpful, I also felt God's presence (for the first time in the same room with Adrian), and I find God's presence an incredible comfort. I methodically explained everything that had occurred: the discussions among the volunteers, our discomfort and requests, and the image I had been seeing in response to prayers. I told the directors about my plea for clarification and God's words to me. Then, I paused to take a breath, and looking Adrian in his vacant eyes, I said, "Adrian, you cannot treat God's people this way. God tasked me to tell you this."

In that moment, a strange thing happened. Adrian's face underwent multiple distortions. I am not talking about him changing expressions. Rather, his physical face contorted in ways I had never seen before except in movies: fluid morphing. I wondered if I was nuts after all. However, afterward, Nancy confirmed that she had also seen the morphing of Adrian's face. I took comfort in the fact that we both had observed this seemingly impossible phenomenon. Later, I wondered if perhaps these facial distortions were a reflection of a fight within Adrian's soul, hopefully nothing more than a reflection of human pride and Adrian's efforts to contain it.

The outcome was definitely worth completing the tasking. I realized that our directors do accept mystical experiences as one way God chooses to communicate. Adrian began conducting the meetings in the Triple S conference room, and a more experienced shift leader came to the meetings to mentor Adrian, whose behavior became more respectful.

Afterward, I questioned whether I was I right in my interpretation of the task and manner of accomplishing it. I wished I had had the opportunity to talk to a spiritual advisor who could have tested the authenticity of the tasking. In the end, everything seemed compellingly clear, but I suppose that could be a deception. Others agreed with my interpretation, but that, too, could be a deception. At least, though, what I had done—properly or improperly—led to a good result for my shift.

There was another positive outcome: Laura, Rebecca, Nancy, and I became friends. We now meet periodically for dinner. I have been blessed with a friendship that likely would not have formed had I not been willing to accept the task to "let Adrian know he cannot treat My people this way."

Moving Forward

After the meeting, I realized that I had no idea how I should relate to Adrian from then on. So, I asked God what to do. In response, I heard two words that absolutely flabbergasted me: "Love him."

Thereupon popped out my usual incredulous response, "Lord, You want me to do *what*? You must be kidding!"

Forgive him? Certainly! But love him? After everything I had been through? Love him when I seem to have been tasked to de-claw him? Love him when he referred to me scathingly and manipulated information about me? Love him when the characteristics that best describe him are ones that repel me? Love him when I felt Evil pulling at him to the point that I recoiled? God is indeed inscrutable! First, God told me to take Adrian to task, and then God told me to love him!

If God said to love him, I realized I would have to learn to do that. I began to pray for Adrian. I began to hug him even though his response was always a cold, mechanical, public gesture. What made the loving easier was knowing for certain that God loves Adrian, just as surely as God loves my mother, so succinctly expressed in the words, "she lives in grace." I suppose that is part and parcel of the new covenant, a pact of love and forgiveness, embodied in the life of Jesus. God has not asked me to give anything that I have not received.

I looked forward to the day that I could enjoy the "delightful peace" that de-Caussade asserts will ensue "when we have learned by faith to find God through all his creatures as through a transparent veil." Although I still sensed a darkness around Adrian, by then I knew that the dark is not overcome by strength and power but rather by love, truth, and a profound weakness that allows the Divine to take over. With time and attitude monitoring, I began to experience love for Adrian as well as gratitude to God for trusting me with this task.

Why Me, Lord?

Ever since coming to faith, I have been grappling with why would God use an atheist. And why would I, the least knowledgeable Catholic around—I peer into the depths of my pool of ignorance every time I teach a catechism class—be tasked to do anything, represent anything, or share my thinking on anything? St. Pio once said, "If God sees blemishes even in the angels, can you imagine what he sees in me?" And I am no saint, like Padre Pio was! Why, then, would God *allow*, let alone *select*, someone like me to do even one task that carried with it a divine mission?

As I stumble around in the "cloud of unknowing," writers I encounter shine inspired rays into the darkness of my unknowing. Two such rays have revealed potential explanations why God might use an atheist for divine purposes.

The first ray came from *The Book of Privy Counseling*: God uses atheists "because He can." That suggestion allowed me to accept not knowing everything I would like to know and to keep on accepting new tasks.

The second ray came from Fr. Richard Rohr's *Things Hidden.* "They [those tasked or used as instruments] are quite flawed or at least ordinary people," writes Fr. Richard, "so it is clear that their power is not their own." That makes sense to me in my currently wide-eyed, occasionally still skeptical, new believer stage of spiritual underdevelopment. Certainly, the events that led to saving the life of Shura and bringing Katya to the United States were well beyond my own power; both cases required not serendipity but a host of people who had not known each other earlier.

Likewise, as St. Paul told the Corinthians (*1 Corinthians* 1: 27-31):

> ²⁷*But God chose the foolish things of the world to shame the wise; God chose the weak things of the world to shame the strong.*
> ²⁸*God chose the lowly things of this world and the despised things— and the things that are not—to nullify the things that are,*
> ²⁹*so that no one may boast before him.*

If an atheist like I was could be used so extensively that some called me "God's agent in Jordan," anyone can be used. That speaks volumes about the power, love, and creativity of God, who can and will help those in need through anyone.

I still don't have a definitive answer, but whether I ever know no longer matters to me here in my "cloud of unknowing," where I have become a part of the droplets that form its endless expanse and they part of me. I feel that I am loved in a deep, humble, and powerful way. Knowledge beyond that is unessential.

The last comment Fr. Thomas Dubay wrote on my note to him was "I rejoice with you." I had not thought of rejoicing, but Fr. Thomas was right. While the tasks sometimes have pushed my abilities to the limit and the Voice always startles me, the intimacy with which God has gifted me is reward beyond compare for obedience.

Contact with Evil

It would appear that if God was with me, protecting me, and raising my siblings and me in response to Danielle's childhood prayer, then Evil was surely not far behind. It would appear that way because we are told that Good and Evil are inseparable. It would also appear that way because of the kinds of experiences I have had.

I do not like to believe that Evil exists. It would be so much easier just to assume that only Good surrounds us, that we can ignore God or accept God but either way Life is Good. That is what I would like to believe. It is what many today believe, and what many in a bygone day believed as well. Beaudelaire in *Les Fleurs du mal* (*The Flowers of Evil*) wrote in the mid-1800s, "My dear Brethren, when you hear the progress of enlightenment extolled, do not forget that the devil's cleverest trick is to persuade you that he does not exist."

Today, according to Loren, Johnson, and Chavda (*Shifting Shadows of Supernatural Power*):

> *"The shifting shadows blurring the lines between light and darkness, good and evil, are creating a twilight zone of spiritual awareness, especially in North America. It results in confusion and apathy on one hand, or an inordinate desire for power at the other extreme. These shadows lead many to call evil 'good' and good 'evil.'"*

Yes, indeed, along with Beaudelaire's "brethren" and my North American compatriots, I would like to believe that Evil does not exist. I would like to ignore those "shifting shadows." It becomes impossible to persevere in this belief and attitude, however, when one is attacked by what would be difficult to label as anything other than Evil.

Bad Things and Good People

When my catechism students ask me, "Why does God let bad things happen to me?," or alternatively, complain when good things happen to individuals they consider bad people, I am reminded of Jeremiah's complaint, "Why do the wicked prosper and the faithless live at ease?" (*Jeremiah* 12:1). In these cases, I try to get the students to think beyond our limited human understanding of fairness and reach toward a greater understanding of our own responsibility for life on this earth and the concept of God's grace as a gift, not a right.

In *When Bad Things Happen to Good People*, Harold Kushner describes God as effete in a chapter titled, "God Can't Do Everything, But He Can Do Some Important Things." While I disagree with Kushner's assessment of God's ability to intervene in our daily lives, I do agree with him that we more often than not pray for the wrong things. We pray for sick people to get well. We pray for peace in the world. My students pray for good grades. What we should be praying for is the strength and guidance to make things better with our own hands as God's servants. I am taken by the prayer, suggested by Jack Riemer (*Likrat Shabbat*) and cited by Kushner:

> *We cannot merely pray to You, O God, to end despair,*
> *For You have already given us the power*
> *To clear away slums and to give hope*
> *If we would only use our power justly.*
> *We cannot merely pray to You, O God, to end disease*
> *For You have already given us great minds with which*
> *To search out cures and healing*
> *If we would only use them constructively.*
> *Therefore we pray to You instead, O God,*
> *For strength, determination, and willpower.*
> *To do instead of just to pray,*
> *To become instead of merely to wish.*

There is something inherently selfish in the question, why has something bad happened to me. Why is it worse for bad things to happen to my relatives or me than to a stranger? God never promised us that we can earn a life of good things happening to us. Quite the contrary: Jesus promised heaven to a co-sufferer who had spent his life as a thief. If we think that we deserve a trouble-free life because we try to be good, then we miss the point, and our prayers become selfish prayers, rather than orations of gratitude for lessons delivered and learned. We become guilty of defining good and bad, security and danger, love and hate, and many other related concepts in profane, rather than sacred, terms. In so doing, we begin to think of man as large and God as small, creating a danger of squeezing God, the will of God, and God's support of free will out of the picture altogether, nursing the hurt that we did not receive what we wanted and thus opening ourselves up to Evil.

If we think that Evil will not target us because we are good or because we are God's people, we miss the fact that Evil is a part of the human-divine equation. When I am asked the question, why is everything going terribly wrong in my life if God loves me, I think of the time that the Voice said to me, "Read *Job*." So many bad things happened to Job, incredibly bad things, any one of which any one of us would lament. Job knew only that the bad things were happening. He did not know why. He had no idea of the Evil behind the bad things. We, too, have no idea that perhaps Evil may be behind some of the bad things that happen to us. The existence of Evil would certainly explain why it seems that more bad things happen to good people than to bad people and why more good things seem to happen to bad people than to good people. After all, Evil would not need to attack bad people. Evil already owns them.

Paranormality

I rarely speak about the paranormal and supernatural experiences in my life, whether paralleling Scripture or coming from something sinister, for fear of being labeled delusional. Yet, they not only have been very real to me, they have often been public in the sense that I was not the only witness. Sometimes the witness was a person totally disconnected from anything paranormal, and the things that happened to me frightened that person.

Interestingly, though, the general population accepts paranomal (e.g., ESP) experiences much more readily than supernatural ones. Yet, are they so different? This is not a rhetorical question. It is a real one, to which I do not know the answer.

Some of these "extra-ordinary" experiences have seemed good; others have seemed bad; yet others appeared to be purely neutral. The good experiences may have predisposed me for ultimate acceptance of the divine supernatural.

The saints tell us that one way to discern God's will is through a sense of peace. If we are acting in accordance with God's will, we should be feeling peaceful about our intentions, and if we are not acting in accordance with God's will, we should be feeling uneasy. However, it is also generally accepted that sometimes Evil will lead us to feel peace when we should be feeling unease.

Likewise, while Loren, Johnson, and Chavda (*Shifting Shadows of Supernatural Power*) state that supernatural power associated with Evil is dark and oppressive and that associated with God light and joyful, they also describe a twilight of co-existence in some cases and confusion as to which is which in others. Good grief! After all the reading I have done, I am left with more questions than answers.

Sorting out the differences between dark forces and God's gifts can numb the mind. Perhaps that is one reason God put me in the Catholic Church. While not everything I have experienced in the way I have experienced it is discussed clearly in weekly homilies, *The Catechism of the Catholic Church* provides some help. Certain practices are identified as inappropriate and not from God:

> *All forms of divination are to be rejected: recourse to Satan or demons, conjuring up the dead or other practices falsely supposed to 'unveil' the future. Consulting horoscopes, astrology, palm readings, interpretation of omens and lots, the phenomena of clairvoyance, and recourse to mediums all conceal a desire for power over time, history, and, in the last analysis, other human beings, as well as a wish to conciliate hidden powers. They contradict the honor, respect, and loving fear that we owe to God alone.*

Equally helpful are the pronouncements of various priests specializing in such matters as cults and exorcism for dioceses. Fr. Lawrence Gesy of the Diocese of Baltimore, having worked with a number of people with ESP and being a consultant to the diocese on cults, suggests that everyone has some psychic abilities, e.g., the mother who instinctively knows what needs to be done to take care of her sick child or who has a sixth sense about her child being in harm's way, something that has happened to me more times than I can count. He also cautions readers of his book, *Today's Destructive Cults and Movements*, about the dangers of assuming that everything supernatural is from God (or saints).

Likewise, Mark Shea ("You Can Trust Me, I'm a Psychic") provides a helpful distinction between dark arts and gifts of God:

> *It is one thing if a person is made the recipient of a supernatural insight or gift (as for instance, St. Bernadette was when the Blessed Virgin appeared to her at Lourdes). It is quite another if a person defies God's express will by seeking supernatural knowledge and power in ways the Lord has expressly forbidden in the First Commandment.*
> *. . . As Saints Peter and Paul say, your adversary the devil prowls around like a roaring lion, seeking someone to devour. And he 'disguises himself as an angel of light' (1 Peter 5:8, 2 Corinthians 11:14).*

Moira Noonan (*Rescued from Darkness: The New Age, Christian Faith, and the Battle for Souls*) relates how she spent 20 years caught in the shadows between good and evil. She gives examples of how God's people of today can get trapped into worshipping false gods just as easily as the people of Israel kept returning to the Canaanite god, Baal.

Sometimes in the past, I believe in retrospect, I was protected from being grabbed and used by dark forces by the same Brazil-nut shell that kept God out. When all my friends were charmed by the Ouija board (a "harmless" game?—perhaps, but more likely not), I walked away in frustration for nothing would make the little pointer move under my hand. I wonder if this is because instead of saying, "yes, yes" (French *oui*; German *ja*), I was mentally saying "no, no." Just as I was unwilling to open my mind consciously to God, I was equally unwilling to open it to the ungod. That, and God's protection, may have prevented me from being swept away into a dark kingdom.

Since I do not understand my experiences with phenomena beyond the physical world enough to examine them adequately or propose a model for analyzing them beyond the principles proposed by the Catholic Church, which I have often found too broad to be helpful in specific cases, I will provide some examples and let you, the reader, be the judge. On a personal basis, I now shun any "gift" unless I know it to be a charism from God, and I don't know that without invoking those tests suggested by St. Teresa. Even so, in some cases, such as those below, I remain confused, and where confused, I have walked away from using the gift, assuming that if God wants me to use it, God will make that clear.

Herein, I believe, lies the key to discerning authenticity of an out-of-the-ordinary charism: an apostolic use for it rather than some form of self-aggrandizement, complacency, hubris, or any kind of personal gain. Fr. John Hardon ("Vision and Visionaries") makes an edifying distinction:

> *Mystics . . . manifest charismatic phenomena. Such phenomena do not occur in the normal development of the spiritual life. They are called charisms because they are given by God for the benefit of others . . . They may be true miracles, like private revelations, divine locutions . . . knowing events at a great distance of space . . . The single most important thing to remember about these charismatic gifts is that they are not for the benefit of the person who possesses them. If genuine, such charismata are always for the benefit of others. They are apostolic and not personal gifts from God.*

Fr. John goes on to point out the crucial dilemma I face in reviewing my past or accepting my present. "What are commonly called mystical phenomena," he writes, "may be produced by persons and forces that are . . . the result of natural psychic powers, or even demonic in their origin." In some cases, where I have been able to help or protect others, I consider that the experiences may well have been Heaven-sent, as in my ability to find Doah on several occasions when he has disappeared. In other cases, where I have known in advance innocuous events, such as Lizzie's encounter with a friend asking for a ride, the seeing of something before it happened may simply have been the realization of a natural psychic ability. In yet other cases, such as my experiences with Tarot, I imagine there were moments when I was standing toe-to-toe with demonic forces, saved from crossing from the light side to the dark because The Light pulled me back even though at the time I was unaware of either the light or the dark and so was entirely at the mercy of God to rescue me.

Finding Doah

Doah had a habit of slinking off, when he wanted to go somewhere and there was no one to take him at precisely the time he wanted to go. It was not the kind of disappearance that a mentally competent child of the same age would make. Rather, it was a matter of marrying "want" with immediate fulfillment, prompted by naïveté and complete trust in the kindness of the surrounding environment that reflects the simplicity of the mentally challenged. Usually, we would find Doah a couple of aisles away in the grocery store, in the backyard on the swing, or at a neighbor's house. Scarier disappearances, however, did occur.

One Sunday morning when Doah was twelve years old but with the mental age and size of a seven-year-old, I emerged from the shower and could not find him. I checked the entire house. No Doah. I checked the backyard. Empty swings. I checked with the all the neighbors. No visit to their homes that day. Panic set in, and I began walking the streets in our subdivision, frantically calling his name. Neighbors I had never before met told me that they knew Doah. Really? He had been wandering farther afield than I had known.

I returned home to Donnie empty-handed. "Why are you losing time by walking all over the neighborhood?" he asked me. "Just think where he is."

"Thinking" referred to what I often "knew" about my children from unexplainable sources. For example, I occasionally "knew" in advance that one or another would get hurt at school, creating a dilemma in that I had no rational way to tell a teacher to be careful and try to prevent the accident. No teacher would have believed me, yet each time the child in question would indeed return home with some minor injury. "Thinking" consisted of emptying my mind and actually *not* thinking at all. If I were sitting quietly, thinking about nothing, sometimes an image would appear of the child, either where the child was at the moment or what would happen to the child in the immediate future.

"Nothing comes to mind about Doah," I told Donnie.

"Just calm down and think for a minute," Donnie repeated.

I took a deep breath, exhaled, and emptied my mind. Blast! In came an image of Doah, clothed in white with a blue belt. He was standing, surrounded by white. White everywhere. Well, one can imagine the worst possible scenario from that.

"I think he's dead," I told Donnie. "Everything around him is white."

"What else?" Donnie pressed, knowing that I am one to miss details. "There has to be more. What is he doing? Is he saying anything? Is there anyone else there?"

Ah! I could not see whether or not there was anyone else there, but he was standing and clapping! Clapping? Church!

In spite of my atheism, Doah had taken up with an evangelical church about a mile from where we lived. Usually, someone would pick him up. That had not happened this time. Still, I *knew* Doah was at the church.

Donnie and I drove to the church apprehensively. What if he were not there? Then what?

I walked in the door and immediately knew I was in the right place. The inside of the church had been painted all white. I wandered through one of the rooms, heard some singing, and moved in that direction. As I turned the corner, I saw another white-walled room, and there in the front row was Doah, standing and clapping, dressed in white clothes, with his blue money belt around his waist. Thank God!

I don't know how to interpret these out-of-the-ordinary experiences in my past. I find it hard to believe that such "help" would come from something demonic. Yet, clearly most parents do not find their missing children by emptying their minds and allowing an image of the location of their children to enter. In some ways, these images presaged how nowadays I approach contemplative prayer. Perhaps back then they reflected God's way of dealing with an atheist in the only way she would (or could) accept. Perhaps they were a charism that I did not recognize as such and am still not sure is such.

I suppose time will tell. In the interim, to those believers who proclaim that they do not accept the supernatural, I would claim that God by God's very nature is supernatural.

Protecting Lizzie

Immediately after Lizzie graduated from high school at the young age of sixteen, she took a job for a year before enrolling in college. When she did not show up after work one day, I fretted about her safety. I had been having a disturbing vision for several weeks. When she had not appeared by early the next morning, I turned her into the police as missing.

Only a few minutes after that, she drove up and explained that the previous evening she had been driving home when she saw a colleague stranded along the roadside with her three children. They lived an hour away, and their car was not functional. So, Lizzie had driven them home. It turned out that their phone was also not functional. Considering that seeking out a pay phone in the middle of the night might involve more risk than she was willing to take, as would driving home alone in the middle of the night, she stayed overnight. She considered my turning her in to the police as missing an overreaction until I related my recurring vision to her.

In this vision, Lizzie was in her car at a stop light at twilight when a very tall African American opened her car door, which she had not locked, and slid into the passenger seat. He pointed a knife at her throat and said, "Take me to the woods." I could have picked out the man in a line-up, so clear was his face to me. I begged Lizzie to try to get home before twilight and under no circumstances to leave her door unlocked.

A few weeks later, Lizzie arrived home rather late from work and told me that my vision had been accurate—sort of. "As usual, Mom," she said, "you got some of the details wrong. You know you are not good at details." (She is right about that.)

"So, okay, I am tooling down Cannery Row, and I have to stop for a red light. And, yeah, I know you told me to keep my door locked, but I forgot. So, while I was waiting for the light to change, along comes this big black dude, opens my door, and gets in the car. It was my friend, Kevin. He pulled out a silver mechanical pencil, pointed it at my neck, and said, 'Take me to Del Rey Woods.' I told him that you told me three weeks ago that he was going to ask this!"

Why I repeatedly saw what turned out to be a rather frivolous event I cannot say. Certainly, I was relieved to hear that the vision had been missing a few important details that turned it from a mother's worst fear to something quite innocuous. At least, the frivolity of this particular vision helped balance out the weightiness of more serious visions. Perhaps it was simply a matter of a mother being closely connected to her children, as Fr. Lawrence Gesy has suggested. With all of my children, from time to time as they were growing up, I would know in advance what was going to happen to them, simultaneously see what they were doing, and even on some occasions, hear what they were thinking. For none of this have I ever been able to find a cogent explanation.

A Face in Moscow

Another vision, occurred on July 18, 1982. I will never forget the date for I will never forget the experience, as shocking as it was curious.

That evening I had just lay down on my University of Moscow bed (actually, a couch that one made up as a bed, with a blanket tucked inside a double-sheet through a triangular opening). After more than a month at the university as part of a summer teacher exchange program, I had grown accustomed to the lumpy bed and would easily have dozed off had I not suddenly seen a face in my window.

I could not place the face although I was certain I knew the brown-eyed woman peering at me from the dark night sky. She seemed to be asking for my help. Unnerved, I jumped up and turned on the light. The pleading face was still there.

Unable to sleep, I knocked on the door of a colleague, a professor from Duke University, with whom I had shared some of my paranormal experiences. His mother had had similar experiences, making him the ideal person to consult in the middle of the night on July 18, 1982.

"Maybe someone in your family is in trouble," he suggested. "Perhaps you should call home."

Now, calling home from the Soviet Union in Cold War times, before the advent of cell phones, required mind-boggling patience and pockets full of rubles. One made a conscious decision to place a call, especially because one had to order the call for a specific time through an operator. I had never called home because of the complexity of doing so, and I knew in this instance I did not need to.

"No, I don't need to call home," I told my colleague. "The face does not belong to anyone in my family. All my children and my husband have blue eyes; I am the only one with brown eyes. No, this is someone else, but I cannot place the person for the life of me."

After a short, rambling discussion that shed no further light on the matter, I shuffled back to my room and tumbled into bed. The matter ended there. The next day I had a full day of studies, which we would be wrapping up in a couple of weeks in order to make an excursion to Leningrad (now St. Petersburg).

The two weeks passed quickly, and soon we found ourselves in St. Petersburg. My roommate, a colleague from Utah, and I parted ways the first day there. I wanted to walk along Nevksy Prospekt and visit the bookstores, as well as walk along the Neva River with its little bridges that open at night for passing ships, a scene not unintentionally reminiscent of Venice. She wanted to visit the Hermitage. We rejoined in the evening to share our experiences.

My roommate returned quite excited. Before she could relate her tourist discoveries, she had something else more important to tell me.

"I ran into one of our friends from Moscow outside the Winter Palace. I could not believe my eyes. What would Zinaida be doing here?"

"Zinaida? Oh, she came here a little over two weeks ago with her kids and husband on vacation, but they were supposed to be back last week. In fact, I called her mother because she was supposed to call me when she got back, but I never heard from her. Her mother did not have any news, either."

"Well, she is here in Leningrad," my roommate offered. "Perhaps she decided to take a slightly longer vacation. Anyway, you will find out tomorrow because she wants you to meet her at 8:00 in front of the Hermitage."

And so at 8:00 the next morning, I walked up to the Hermitage. There stood Zinaida, her husband, and their kids. Zinaida had her back to me, so one of the children saw me first and called out. Zinaiada turned around, and there I saw it: the face in my window. It was Zinaida's face!

After we exchanged the ritual three kisses on the cheek, I asked Zinaida where she had been on the night of July 18. Her response confirmed my conclusion and floored me at the same.

"We were fleeing Moscow," she said. "My neighbor had been arrested for church activity [illegal during the days of communism]. Because we belong to the same Orthodox church, I feared for the safety of my family. We were going on vacation, as planned, but I knew we would not return to Moscow from our vacation. I was thinking so strongly about you. I wanted so badly to contact you."

"Well, you did contact me," I told her. I related to her the vision I had seen of her in my window. She, in turn, was floored.

By the time I had reached Leningrad, she had plans underway to emigrate. A German friend had stepped up to the plate to help her, so my help, so urgently desired the night of July 18, turned out not to be needed. For that, I was relieved because I was a lowly graduate student with no way to help her other than through moral support and perhaps making connections with others who could help (something I did for one dissident who was thereafter able to escape).

Once again, I do not know how to interpret this event. I would not label it as either good or bad. It was a neutral experience in which one human being, who happened to be Russian Orthodox, reached out to another human being, who happened to be an American atheist. What was this all about?

The *Catholic Encyclopedia* says that there are more instances of this kind of event than would be accounted for by chance, yet insufficient evidence exists to confirm any theory. So, I guess, no one knows. At least, not now, not yet. Nonetheless, I find myself wanting to connect my later mystical experiences with these earlier unexplainable paranormal events.

When Tarot Does Not Lie

I do not have to ask whether or not there is a dark side to reading Tarot cards. The *Bible* is very clear on that issue. *Deuteronomy* 18: 10-12 tells us that anyone who practices divination is detestable to God. Likewise, throughout the *Bible* occult arts are condemned (see, for example, *2 Kings* 21: 6 and a number of other places, including the first commandment).

Being detestable to God did not concern me during the years that I read Tarot cards for at that time I was convinced that there was no God. I was also convinced that the Tarot was quite a useful thing: every card layout I ever read brought an accurate prediction, contrary to the assertion of Wiseman (*Paranormality*), who contends that Tarot layouts reflect mere hit-and-miss coincidence. That was not so in my experience. For example, a friend of mine became very unhappy in her job when it took a turn in a direction that she felt was not good for her and not good for her institution. She loved the job itself but not the direction in which the management was moving. Stay or quit? She was torn. Twice I laid out the cards for her. Twice they indicated that she should quit the job. She stayed with it for a while, then decided to quit. She told me years later that the cards had accurately shown the best decision for her.

Another person for whom I laid out cards was my roommate during the days I was working at NASA in the late 1990s. She was the ex-wife of an Apollo astronaut and had a neighbor she detested because of his arrogance and cruelty. She asked me to lay out the Tarot about how life would treat him in the future. The layout was grim.

"Something really bad is going to happen to him," I told her. "Something worse than he has ever experienced before." That was in the evening. The next morning he had a stroke that left him paralyzed.

Along lighter lines, she wanted to know if she were ever going to get remarried. The cards said yes, but the timeline was very unclear. Year after year passed without her ever so much as meeting a prospect. Then, I lost track of her for a couple of years. When she found me again, she sent me an exclamatory letter, triumphing her recent marriage. "The cards were right," she wrote. She had never forgotten that layout.

It was another layout, though, that I never forgot. I was asking a variety of future-oriented questions with a friend when I felt one of the cards, not yet overturned, absolutely burning under my hand. At the same time, I saw an image of my father-in-law sitting in a chair outside the window on the lawn, looking woebegone. I jerked back as if I had been burned.

"What's the matter?" asked my friend.

"This card is red hot!"

"Turn it over. Let's see which card it is."

I turned it over. "It's the Emperor."

"Who is the Emperor?" asked my friend. We had assigned people we know to each of the Tarot cards, which is one way of reading more into them than the layout of the Celtic cross alone, which we were using, would give.

"I don't remember. You have the list." I looked over to where she had placed the list, and she picked it up.

"It's your father-in-law," she said.

That was too much of a coincidence—my father-in-law on the lawn, looking bedraggled and sitting painfully in a chair, and my father-in-law burning under my hand. I picked up the phone and called my mother-in-law.

She was shocked by my call. "I cannot believe that you are calling me," she exclaimed. "I just walked in the door. Dad [I always called him that] had a heart attack earlier tonight, and he is scheduled for his second quadruple bypass as soon as they stabilize him, probably in the morning." I did not tell her what had happened with the Tarot cards. I simply wished them both well, promised to tell Donnie, and hung up.

The hour being late and the events of the evening not inducing me to involve myself in any more Tarot reading for that day, I said goodnight to my friend, with whom I was staying, and wearily walked down the hall to her guest bedroom. As I lay down and before I nodded off, in that dim twilight between wakefulness and sleep, I saw a door to which I felt drawn. In my mind, I walked over to the door, opened it, and, seeing a downward spiraling staircase, began to descend when I felt an overpowering desire to escape. That desire pulled me from near-sleep, shaking. Fully awake, I knew with whom I needed to speak: my brother, Willie.

Willie had an incredible ESP gift, and he was the best reader of Tarot around our farm community. His predictions always came true, but he stopped reading Tarot after the death of one of his school chums, the circumstances of which he had predicted with great precision. After he came to faith a number of years earlier, he burned his hand-painted cards.

Willie had also dabbled in mild forms of the occult if any forms of the occult can be considered mild. These were things that I would not touch. They frightened and repelled me. I felt a strong danger in them. When I related the experience of the evening to him, his voice took on a guarded and directive tone. He was clearly concerned about his oldest sister, but as if to protect me, he never did tell me everything that he thought had occurred.

"Right now, stop!" he pleaded. "No more Tarot. Never. You cannot touch those cards again. That door is a dangerous one. You should never have opened it."

"Where does it lead?" My natural curiosity often tempts me to take risks that wiser folks would not.

"You do not want to know where it leads," was all he would say. Well, it led downward. That much I knew.

"Guess whatever you want to guess," he concluded, "but do not go there. You have no idea what you are getting into. I have been there. I am lucky to have made it out."

To this day, I am not certain what was really going on, but I am certain that Willie understood more than I do and that he had experienced something very dark and dangerous that started out not unlike my opening that door.

I followed Willie's advice. Well, at least in part. My desire to open that door disappeared entirely, and had the opportunity to explore further popped up—thank God, it did not—I would have walked away from it. As for the Tarot cards, I stopped reading them, but I kept them on a shelf until after I, too, came to faith, at which time, I trashed them. On an intuitive, inexpressible level, I realized finally that I had been treading on some very dangerous ground.

The *Bible* (Old Testament and the writings of St. Paul) tells us that only God has the right to reveal the future. So, if the Tarot cards revealed the future accurately to me, then the source of that knowledge had to come from the dark side. I have sometimes wondered if Evil helped me out back then in order to keep me an atheist. Was that door an invitation into the dark realms? What pulled me back from it, given my inordinate curiosity that in the physical world has nearly led to my demise upon occasion? How did an atheist know to avoid the descent?

In asking these questions, I cannot help but think of Danielle's prayer, asking God to raise us. Had God's protection saved Willie? Was it God who pulled me back up that staircase and into wakefulness?

Possessed?

My brother, Rollie, too, had ESP experiences. Nearly all my siblings have had them. Whether these were an escape mechanism, the result of beatings, or simply something we were born with, I cannot say. We have had the ability to predict some things, the ability to hear others' thoughts, and the ability to know things that are not seen and to see things that are not known, along with other experiences that seem to come from another, non-three-dimensional universe. Of all of us, Rollie had the most frightening experience with the dark side, and we all witnessed it.

Rollie recalls very vividly how Evil entered his body. A house painter, he was finishing a house late one night and opened the door to the basement. A deep voice from the basement called to him, "What do you want? Power? Money? The envy of men? I can give it all to you!"

This was a useless question because Rollie, like me, is not attracted by power and could care less about money. As long as we have a roof over our heads (it could be a tent for all we care), food to eat upon occasion (does not even have to be every meal), and work to do (even if the work is of our own making), we are happy. Possessions are meaningless to us, and as for the envy of man, we neither desire to be envied nor do we envy anyone; it is not in our nature. I think we are just happy that we survived our abusive childhoods with our life, limbs, and mental health intact. We both count our riches only in the people we have helped.

Rollie answered the voice, "Hell, I don't want any of that" and tried to shut the door when he felt a force enter through his feet all the way to his chest and begin to speak in another voice. He threw down all his equipment and rushed home.

From home, he called me, screaming over and over in a deep, horror-film voice, "Beth! Beth! Pick up! It's Rollie! I need you! Beth! Pick up, please!"

Finally, the racket coming across the answering machine did awaken me. So strange and unfamiliar was the voice that I did not know who or what was calling out to me or what was wanted from me. All I knew was that this was *not* Rollie even though the phone number shown on the answering machine was his and he had self-identified. It took several more pleas before I realized that it *was* Rollie talking. (Later, Rollie's wife told me that she had not recognized his voice, either, nor did she recognize the man who lived with her for the next three months.)

I spent some time coaxing Rollie out from behind that other voice. The only description of it I can give is that it sounded like a dead man talking. It was not Rollie, yet somewhere Rollie was in his own body and reaching out to me for help.

I thought at the time that he must be suffering from some type of schizophrenia, but he claims that he was possessed, that he was in his body more as an observer than as the owner, and that he knew the person who caused the possession: a man named Bill, whom he had crossed at work. He had seen Bill about a week before this happened, and Bill had made some kind of threat about his soul. A few days after it happened, Bill asked him how his soul was faring.

Our sister, Victoria, who also has the gift (or curse) of ESP, met Bill and was frightened. She felt that he was not exactly a living being, that he had "dead eyes."

As an atheist, I was not much help to Rollie even though I, as his oldest sister, was the first person he called as the one to whom most of my siblings come for advice. Elimination of this being controlling Rollie was beyond my ability. So, Rollie called Danielle, and every day for three months she prayed with him, not caring in the least about his espoused atheism.

Ultimately, it was a meeting with Bill that chased away Rollie's demon. Bill told Rollie that he had happily sold his own soul—he was quite wealthy, and his wealth was what he claimed to have received in return—and asked Rollie what would be the price for his soul. Rollie's response was that he did not have a price, but Bill pushed, saying that everyone has a price. Finally, Rollie, realizing that he was not going to be left alone until he gave a figure, said he did have a price. Bill asked what it was, and Rollie responded "one on one."

"What do you mean by that?" Bill asked.

"You release every soul you have ever captured," Rollie said, "and you and I spend eternity alone, one on one." Whatever was controlling Rollie's body left. Immediately.

Regardless of how much of this experience was real and how much of it was perceived is less important than one fact: Rollie was willing to sacrifice himself for others. That may be what ultimately saved him from what possessed him, if indeed, he was possessed. I think, too, there must be cases where God steps in, as with Job, and says, "enough is enough."

Rollie's story is not the classic case of possession, the type one hears about when one speaks about exorcism. Possession, we are told, cannot happen without a person's consent, and for three months Rollie refused to consent.

That this should happen to Rollie, who believes in neither God nor Satan, seems unlikely, yet it happened. Malachi Martin, in *Hostage to the Devil*, warns that more instances like this can occur simply because we as a nation, perhaps even as a world community, generally do not believe in evil. He says:

> *The belief that he [Lucifer] does not exist at all is an enormous advantage that he has never enjoyed to such a great degree. It is the ultimate camouflage. Not to believe in evil is not to be armed against it. To disbelieve is to be disarmed. If your will does not accept the existence of evil, you are rendered incapable of resisting evil. Those with no capacity of resistance become prime targets for possession.*

Rollie must have been one of those prime targets, given his philosophical outlook. Fortunately, his willingness to sacrifice himself for others made him a poor home. More than that I cannot guess, and very little do I claim to know.

Why did Rollie not need an exorcist to escape from the clutches of whatever it was that had a stranglehold on him? Was he perhaps not really possessed? Was he somehow protected, beginning from the days of Danielle's prayer for God's intercession in our rearing? Was he saved through the efforts of the 8-pack, in this case Danielle, because the 8-pack was the instrument of choice for God to use?

While what happened to Rollie interfered with living a normal life, whether or not his experience could be labeled true possession, I am not qualified to say. Unfortunately, the information available on possession is contradictory. Henri Gesland writes that out of 3000 consultations on possession, "there have been only four cases of what I believe to be demonic possession." T. K. Osterreich, on the other hand, claims "possession has been an extremely common phenomenon, cases of which abound in the history of religion." Martin puts these extremes into perspective: "The truth is that official or scholarly census of possession cases has never been made."

This lack of clarity makes the interpretation of Rollie's experience very difficult, if not impossible. Moreover, Martin states that in his experience and in the knowledge base of the Catholic Church, possession is not a rapid change of state but something that occurs slowly over time as if one had left a door open a crack and in seeps evil until finally it is fully inside and in control of the house. For Rollie, however, what happened was swift and immediate. His experience was less a possession of the classical type and more an occupation, not unlike a mirror reflection of the divine occupation I experienced, but clearly not divine in origin. I assume that Evil, like Good, does not need to follow rules established by men or patterns perceived by holy bodies over the centuries but can proceed at will, that either *can* do whatever either wants simply because both have the power to do so, the latter being held in check only by the former and the former existing outside the realm of any limitations.

Something happened to Rollie. It was not good. In the end, it simply moved out. More than that, I can only make suppositions about the nature of the thing, and those suppositions might be as wrong as they might be right. As in the case of the topic of Evil in general, the reading I have done on the issue of demonic possession, when transposed with what I know of Rollie's experience, raises more questions than it answers. What matters is that before it became too late, Good intervened, and Rollie became whole again.

Rollie's experience reinforces my sense that God did answer Danielle's prayer to raise us because all of the 8-pack, the two atheists included, developed a deep morality that led Rollie to be willing to sacrifice himself for others, that led all of us to be willing to suffer whatever humility might be necessary to put others first, forgive those who harmed us, and carry out divine taskings when we had no idea where they were coming from or what harm we would incur from doing so. Given the abusive, totalitarian environment in which we grew up, who else could have taught us that? To say the atheists among us had no moral compass would be true but to say we had no moral barometer would be equally untrue.

Attacks

Whether I was attacked by Evil as an atheist, I do not know. I may not have recognized an attack had there been one. On the other hand, maybe Evil was comfortable with me the way I was. After all, I was not a threat.

After my conversion, however, a couple of events happened that were difficult to ignore or to pass off as anything other than Evil in action. Considering that I am by nature oblivious to what goes on around me, it is perhaps not so amazing that the ways in which I have felt attacked by Evil post-conversion have been overt and growingly forceful.

A Special Passenger

Twice, not long after my conversion, as I left work alone late at night, I distinctly felt as if someone were sitting in the back seat of my car. Both times I whipped around and saw no one but still felt a dark presence. In the event that it might be something of an evil sort, for that is precisely what it felt like, I spoke aloud, "Whoever you are, please do not skulk about in the back seat. Come up front with me and sit in the passenger seat. We can pray together all the way home because that is what I intend to do."

Each time, no sooner had I finished speaking than the sense of darkness and evil dissipated. Obviously, praying together was not part of the plan.

Both of these events occurred in the same week. That was a few years ago. Since my second offer to pray together, I have never sensed an unwanted passenger again.

Stalked

In taking one of my diurnal perambulations around the grounds of Old Mission in San Ignatio, I walked up to the door of the mission church to talk to God; that is where I like to do the talking part of prayer. As I did so, I heard a sound like someone walking behind me, then sensed someone, maybe 5-6 inches taller than I, standing beside me. It startled me because I had thought I was alone. I looked to my left, from where I had heard the sound, and saw a black space, like a breathing shadow, roughly proportionate to a human being's dimensions. I jumped, at first thinking it was a person, perhaps one not with the best of intentions, then noticed that it was nothing but black air. Overwhelmed by confusion, I quickly walked away, spooked. Then, I realized that this might be something evil, trying to prevent me from praying or from being close to God. I was *not* going to let that happen. I immediately turned around and came back though the "thing" was still hanging around. It did not touch me, so I said my prayer and walked back to the path when I heard the sound of someone stepping on dry leaves. I turned around and saw a cracked leaf on the ground but no one anywhere in the vicinity.

I figured that this must be what people call Evil—Satan or a demon, something supernatural and not good, anyway. I don't know why, but it made me really mad that *my* mission had been invaded this way. I found it hard to believe that God would permit evil to be that close to this sanctuary. In anger, I confronted the thing. "How *dare* you intrude on God's place?" I demanded to know. "You do not belong here. The mission is God's, not yours. Go where you belong. Get away from here. This is God's ground, and you have no right to be here!" The sense of this evil presence departed. I felt no fear, only indignation. More than anything I wanted to protect this prayer-soaked place, God's place, from intrusion.

When coming to faith, I had given no thought to the possibility of the existence of Evil. I would like to think that there is no Evil One, but my experience at the mission has caused me to think otherwise.

Nightmares

For some time now, I have no longer been attacked in the open, at least not that I have been aware of. (I am conscious of the fact that Evil can attack in sweet, seductive ways that may not be perceived as evil in nature, and I have to assume that I am as susceptible to those as anyone else and try to improve my ability to discern the nature of the experiences and temptations that are in front of me). While the open attacks subsided, ones more difficult to repel began to occur.

About six months post-conversion, I began to have deeply disturbing, dark, godless nightmares, which I interpreted as Evil's way to reach me when I was at my most vulnerable: asleep. Now, I am not a person who knows how to be sleepless. Although I sleep, on the average, fewer total hours than the average person, I fall asleep easily and sleep soundly. No one can wake me for any reason when I am asleep, a problematic trait when my kids were small. Donnie was always the one to tend them if they became ill at night..

When the nightmares struck, I knew I could not handle them on my own, so I turned the dilemma over to God, praying that my dreams be filled only with thoughts of the Divine. The first night I prayed for that, the nightmares did not appear. I awoke refreshed, with the sense that my dreams had been wonderful. (With the exception of those black nightmares, I have rarely been able to remember details from my dreams.)

My skeptical self might question whether I had turned off the nightmares on my own by willing myself not to dream them. However, research shows that this is highly unlikely. Harvard psychologist Daniel Wegner conducted experiments in controlling dreams. He found that not wanting to dream about something invariably ensured that the person would dream about it. My experience with these nightmares has convinced me that while people may not be able to control their dreams, most assuredly God can.

The second night that I prayed that my dreams be filled only with thoughts of God, the nightmares did not appear. Again, I awoke refreshed, with the sense that my dreams had been wonderful. Since then, I have prayed for dreams only of God every single night, and every single night since then God has answered that prayer. For that, I continue to express abundant gratitude.

A friend who read this manuscript shared with me a prayer ascribed to St. Pio although it may not actually be his. It seems that St. Pio was also attacked by demons in his sleep. He is said to have prayed the following words, which are so significantly more elegant than any I could devise that I have borrowed them for nightly use:

> *Lord Jesus Christ, my God, I adore you and thank you for all the graces you have given me this day. I offer you my sleep and the moments of the night. I beseech you to protect me and keep me safe. Therefore, I place myself within your sacred side and under the mantle of our Blessed Lady. Let all your holy angels stand about me and keep me in your peace. Let your blessings be upon me throughout the hours of this night, so I may awake to serve you, strengthened and refreshed for a new day.*

God seems always to answer this particular prayer. For that, I am deeply grateful, and I tell God that.

God at Work

I work in a position that demands separation of church and state. Bringing God into the workplace is not only difficult, it is forbidden. Nonetheless, I have found that I cannot shut the door on God when I cross the threshold into my office. God being in the workplace with me makes a difference not only in the way I do my job but also in my spiritual development. After all, how can we grow in our relationship with anyone—God, friends, family—if we persevere in our daily activities without acknowledging their presence? All activities become more enjoyable and meaningful when shared with God in the doing of them.

Then and Now

I have always tried to be a good boss, to support and empower employees. However, there is a different feel to my experiences before and after conversion.

Before conversion, I had an excellent reputation for running a successful enterprise where people excelled at their occupations and expressed satisfaction with their work environment. They felt empowered, primarily because I learned how to delegate, mentor, and support. People bonded to me, sometimes through fighting together against idiocies of the establishment and other times through shared vision. I knew little about people's personal lives. I considered that proper at the time. After all, we were at work to accomplish a professional mission, and we did that successfully. What more could a leader want?

After conversion, I have earned an excellent reputation for running a successful enterprise where people excel at their occupations, are clearly happy in their work environment, and at peace in general. They say they feel empowered because they know I trust them, care about them, and will take the time needed to develop them. People are bonded not only to me but also to each other. While there are frustrations and the establishment sometimes takes some stances that appear idiotic to us, our bonds are not built in an us-against-them effort but in a loving approach that takes as the starting point the conviction that everyone in our organization wants the mission to succeed and is basically a good person, that every person is needed and essential, and that we all need each other in special ways at special times. I know a lot about people's personal lives now. Employees use my open door policy not just to discuss work issues but also to share their personal concerns, insecurities, philosophies, needs, desires, and friendship. They even, at times, ask for prayer; those who are Christians sometimes want me to pray with them on the spot. (For that matter, both Muslims and Jews have asked me to pray for them.) Employees talk to me about their families, their colleagues, and, in surprisingly more cases than one might think, regardless of their brand of religion, about their relationship with God. That is proper in an organization where God's presence is welcomed. We have had to pray often for one colleague or another, and we have had more than our share of miracles.

I have found the answer to my pre-conversion question, what more could a leader want? A leader could want God's presence in building the house and guarding the city. In earlier days, an organization I built without God's help was dismantled by human hands four years later. The organization I am currently building with God's help may also be dismantled by human hands at some point in the future (although with 125% growth every year for the past five years, I don't think that is going happen any time soon). If it is, what will not be dismantled is the house we are all building together with God's help. Some employees have retired during the past five years and some have moved on to other positions that pay more; most have stayed in touch and are still willing to lend a helping hand, a sympathetic ear, or a plaintive prayer. A foundation has been laid that supports not just the work mission but also, and more important, our human needs.

The Job God Wanted for Me

I had been happily working in Jordan, a wonderful country—ancient, holy in history, and friendly—when I got a fateful call from a former boss. He had just been selected as CEO and was asking me to apply to come back to the States and work as one of his four direct reports. If selected, I would be responsible for nationwide and international operations. It was intriguing, but I was already working internationally, shuttling between Bahrain and Jordan in order to help out the division in Bahrain, which had lost its head person, and doing occasional consulting in any one of two dozen other countries. I wavered, mostly drawn toward the *status quo.*

Then, my boss in Jordan, an Egyptian of grand proportions and even greater pride and temper, he for whom I was told not to pray, learned about the phone call, and the full fury of an Arab slighted fell upon me, loyalty being the number one trait that, in my experience, Arabs expect from friends and employees. He tore up my contract. He would not allow me to leave him on my own. The only way I would be leaving would be if he sent me away, and he was doing just that.

It was odd that he found out about the phone call. Only two people knew, and both insisted that they had not told. It does not matter who, if either, told. My boss would have found out, anyway, because God wanted me back in the USA in the proffered position. With the passage of time, that became clear although the why of it did not.

My position in Jordan ended peacefully. I had already been paid for the quarter, so I got a 3-month vacation. My boss left for Egypt and returned a month later, calmer. We met. In the Arab way, we drank tea before broaching serious matters and then settled down to discussing "the situation." I asked why he thought I would choose the USA over Jordan; I might very well have chosen Jordan over the USA. He seemed puzzled about that at first, talked about how I was "leaving him" (I was right about the loyalty issue), and finally commented that he would be in his hotel room until the morning if anything else came up that I would like to talk about. We parted civilly. I felt sadness from him. Months later, I realized that in the Arab manner of saving face he was letting me know that he would like me to come back but that I would have to be the one to take the first step. I knew that. I had lived in the culture long enough to read between the lines, but I did not. I took everything at face value in the American way. Why? I have been called a "cultural chameleon;" I am known for being good at understanding unspoken communication in other cultures, yet I failed to recognize something that I knew very well. Did God cloud my thinking because there was that job I am supposed to have in the USA?

I, however, did not want that job. I began rapidly opening doors in Jordan, and I had much help. I had acquired enough respect there for being a good professor and a good administrator to receive a number of job offers. I taught at the University of Jordan fall semester, but spring semester was adequately staffed, leaving no possibility of continuation.

In fact, every door I opened in Jordan was closed. Every person who tried to help me moved unexpectedly. Seriously. One professor and one administrator were moved by their organization to Bahrain. One dean was recycled back into the faculty, and immediately after that, he had the opportunity to teach in Lebanon; off he went.

In the interim, I kept being pushed in less than subtle ways toward the USA job, which began to look better. Actually, it was a very good job. While I was hesitating, the salary offer increased by 20%. That sweetened the pot. Then, I coincidentally(?) ended up at a conference with the senior leadership from the US organization, ran into them by chance, and socialized a while. They urged me to put in my papers. I did—one day before the deadline. I was interviewed and shortly thereafter a job offer was made. At the same time, Donnie's contract in Jordan was terminated. When God says "no," God means "no." So, with the USA job offer being the only one I had in spite of never before having had any trouble cultivating job offers, back we came to California.

After two years of working in my current position, I began looking for another job for several reasons: (1) the lure of a promotion and higher wages and (2) a bit of an ethical dilemma associated with one of the projects I supervised—I disagreed strongly with the position of the organization. Once again, I quickly found another opportunity, a vice president position close enough to home that I would not have to move and with a salary that represented a significant raise. I was one of the top three candidates, and on a Wednesday I interviewed for the position. The vibes from the interview were good, and I assessed my chances of landing the job as strong.

Clearly, however, God had put me in my current position and wanted me to stay there. Things started happening again.

First, every single day about once an hour one employee after another would come into my office, tell me how much they liked working with me, explain how much I belong here where I am, and share a story of some difference I had made in his or her life. Here was something I had not considered. I began to feel a long-term obligation to these people.

Second, on the Saturday after the interview and knowing nothing about my job search, our former parish priest showed up at my door with an article related to the ethical dilemma I was facing, one for which Fr. Louis Vitale, a Franciscan activist and friend of our priest, had spent time in jail. I had discussed the situation with our priest earlier; he was my spiritual barometer. He told me that he thought that I was in a very good position to help the ethical dilemma be resolved and that I should keep this in mind whenever I was troubled about it. (He was stunned to hear about the job interview, i.e. my attempt to escape the situation.) Our priest turned out to be right. My staff and I *were* able to ameliorate the ethical dilemma.

Third, just to make sure that I had no choice (because sometimes I have to get conked on the head in order to see God's beckoning hand), the job for which I had interviewed went away. Poof! The Board of Directors decided that they did not need an executive vice president, given the current economic climate. As with Jonah, who had run away from Ninevah but ultimately was thrown upon its shore by a whale inexorably bringing him back to where God had sent him, God brought me right back to where God wanted me to be, right where I am now.

It would seem that here is where God wants me. I will therefore be here until directed elsewhere. My Jonah period is over.

Of course, temptations continue to arise. When our last Executive Director left and our current Executive Director arrived, we threw both of them a party. At that party, I met an old friend from Washington, D.C., Dobbin. Dobbin was getting ready to retire from his influential, well paid position and asked me if I might consider moving on from my current position. He went on to tell me that there were not one, but *three*, positions of high status and big money in Washington about to open up. He told me that all three incumbents would like me to be their successor.

Certainly, the money would have be much better than I was earning, and opportunities for moonlighting and consulting would be much more plentiful. So, from the point of view of salary and what it would buy—a comfortable retirement, a luxurious home, money to travel, nice stuff, an inheritance for the children—these opportunities were enticing.

From the point of view of excitement and rubbing shoulders with national power mongers, just thinking about these positions brought a rush of ambitious headiness. I would be associating with the people about whom one reads in the national news.

Now, that brings a great sense of importance! Self-efficacy, self-esteem! Confidence and pride! (So much for Franciscan humility!)

From the point of view of making a national contribution, the work would have an impact. I could leave a legacy, see my name in print, make my kids proud.

Dobbin suggested that I drop by the next time I was in Washington, preferably soon. Neat! I floated home on a heady cloud and wisped up to Donnie, giving him the great news.

He looked at me quizzically, "Would you really want to move away from San Ignatio? I would not trade San Ignatio for Washington."

Oh, yeah, that! I would have to leave my prayer-soaked town for a city of neon and naughtiness. No, I did not want to do that. Not really. The town I live in is the place God planted me. The job I have is the job God chose for me. After my previous thwarted attempt at leaving this job, I had made a commitment to God to be here. Thoughts about the Washington positions created feelings of excitement. Thoughts about my current position, San Ignatio, and Old Mission brought feelings of peace and belonging. I think that is what discernment is about—determining where God wants us—and God has made that easy for me.

I suppose if I had tried to fly away from here, God would have closed those positions in the same way that the ones I found earlier disappeared. I like to think, though, that it was much better to turn my back on the temptation on my own. So, good-bye, big money. For what did I need you, anyway? My current job will give me a comfortable retirement. I really don't need much to be happy. A luxurious home creates the need to spend more time in caring for it than in other more important endeavors, such as caring for the homeless. Money to travel? Puh-leez! My current job has me up in the air most of the time. Nice stuff? And just what am I supposed to do with it? An inheritance for the children? We have already given the family sentimental objects and heirlooms to them. As far as any large monetary sums are concerned, that is not the kind of inheritance I want to give them. I want to leave them diligence, self-reliance, knowledge, capabilities, parenting skills, study skills, concern for neighbor more than self, and good character, along with a sense of joy, peace, and love, i.e. the ability to make their own inheritance. Beyond that, they are God's to take care of.

But wait, what about that great sense of self-importance and self-esteem that comes from rubbing shoulders with the powerful? Oh, right, I am already important as a child of God, and there is no one more powerful than God with whom I could possibly rub shoulders. Anything more is illusion and hubris.

I don't need to see my name in the press, and as for my kids, they are already proud of me just the way I am, just as I am proud of them just the way they are. There is nothing lacking after which I have to chase across an entire continent. Better to remain still and enjoy all that I have right here.

As I reflected on the negative aspects of leaving, it was easy to see the immense treasure I have right where I am. Most of my children are just a few minutes away. My support, too, has been here in the humble folk in my prayer group, in the naive teens in my catechism class, and in the yearning-for-understanding townspeople in my Bible sudy class. Good people. God's people.

Fortunately, it only took a few minutes for me to see the potential job offers for what they were: a temptation to move away from where God put me, a step back from the tasks God had given me, and the likelihood of surrounding myself with people other than those to whom God brought me. I still understand imperfectly, but I do know that here is where I am to be. Therefore, here is where I will be.

God Works Here, Too

One morning I encountered complications in getting into work and called my new assistant, Dr. Warren, asking him to take charge and to let the CEO know I had been unable to reach him. Dr. Warren emailed the CEO, ending his note with the words, "God help us all because Beth won't be in this morning and I, Dr. New Guy, will be responsible for all activities."

When I made it in, Dr. Warren showed me the note he had received from the CEO in response. The CEO had written that he was not at all worried about our division because "God always helps Beth and the people in your division!"

The CEO is right. God does help us. One junior manager, upon accepting the directorship of another division, ended his farewell note to me with the words, "Blessed are those who have you as their leader for they shall do their work well." From his note, it seems that those who work in our division sense the spirituality here as God continues to spoil my colleagues and me. Of that, I have many examples. Some are ways in which God helps me be a better leader; yet others God grants in answer to prayer. And then, of course, there are those infamous times when I, in a not-humble moment, begin to think that I personally have something to do with the success of our programs and God shows me how wrong I am.

Inspection!

Recently, inspectors came from Washington to look at our programs for quality assurance. I was unable to meet with them because of previously scheduled events, so I had them meet with our senior managers, whom I trust implicitly. The head inspector subsequently insisted that my secretary find time for her to meet with me. My secretary pulled me out of a meeting to determine when, if at all, I could do this. The inspector seemed nervous and really desirous of time with me, not with someone else, so I told my secretary to move my early afternoon appointment to after work, which was possible given the people involved. The inspector gratefully thanked me and showed up promptly for her appointment.

When she entered my office, she closed the door and asked to speak confidentially. She did not want to talk about our division. Rather, she described management problems on her own team that had befuddled and distressed her. She wanted advice. Oh, my! I said a quick silent prayer for guidance, then brainstormed the situation with her. She liked the approach that emerged, thanked me for my "mentorship," and left in peace.

I spent a few stunned moments with God afterward. God's presence at work never fails to take the most unusual turns.

Arrogance

Just when I begin to take God at work for granted and, even worse, begin to think that I myself create our harmonious work climate, God shows me vividly who is really in charge. For example, I once had to transfer an employee to another division. Since most employees do not want to transfer out of my division (this is a good thing), I usually am the one to deliver them the bad news. Health is the most frequent reason for transferring individuals out of my division since all my employees must be able to travel frequently.

So, given a situation where an employee had developed some serious health problems, the program manager had made the decision to transfer him to a division doing similar work but not requiring travel. This looked to be an open-and-shut case. The employee did not want to travel and would not sign the annual paperwork, agreeing to travel. No need to pray about this one! Piece of cake!

When I met with the program manager and the employee, however, the employee turned hostile, demanding that we grant him an exception to policy. He threatened to reveal documents he claimed to have on each of us that would make us do whatever he wanted us to do.

Later in the day, he brought a sealed envelope to my secretary. In it was a copy of some personal correspondence I had had with another employee that could be misconstrued. He had obtained the file when the other employee's computer had been broken and the two employees had shared one computer. The correspondence was innocent enough but out of context could become embarrassing. The employee in question, seemingly a docile individual, had retained that correspondence for more than four years, apparently holding it for a time that he could use it to compel me to do something that he wanted to have done. The time had come. Blackmail!

The employee miscalculated. As a rugged individualist from New England, to use Emerson's archetypal image, I do not respond to blackmail. In fact, had I been wavering about perhaps granting an exception, the attempted blackmail sealed the fate of the individual in question: he would be transferred without delay.

Since blackmail is a felony, punishable by heavy fines and imprisonment, I was confronted with a difficult decision: to prosecute or not to prosecute. Employees who blackmail employers under California law generally lose their jobs. The employee might be terminated if I shared the situation with our human resources and legal staffs. If I did not share the information, I might end up having lost the opportunity for defense later, but the employee, who was elderly, in poor health, and responsible for a family with serious medical problems, would not lose a job he desperately needed and a salary that he could not replicate. Did I take the risk of professional damage or did I take the route of hurting the employee?

I, too, had miscalculated. Even in seemingly small things, I do need God's help and presence. Not praying about all of it is arrogance. Thinking I can handle any part of it is evidence of my lack of humility and my continuing need to develop more.

Realizing my mistake, over the weekend I asked God to guide me in the decision whether or not to prosecute the employee for blackmail. I felt no guidance all weekend. On Sunday, I missed the morning Mass. Doah had wanted to go with me but did not call until too late. By the time he called, it was too late even for the noon Spanish Mass. However, there was an evening Mass in a church in the town where he lives. So, we made arrangements to go there.

When I entered the church with Doah, I was hoping that God would use something in the readings, music, or homily to provide guidance because I certainly would have to make a decision the next day. It was more a matter of expectant waiting and not stress. I have learned the lesson well that once I give a problem to God, I don't have to worry about it anymore.

Nothing in the readings or music provided any help with my difficult decision. So, I settled in to listen carefully to the homily. It was short, but good—and had nothing to do with my situation. The homily was short because the priest could barely speak. He had been in Latin America, where he caught bronchial pneumonia, was hospitalized, and then put on long-term bed rest. As a result, he had returned two months late to the parish. Although regularly taking antibiotics, he still suffered from bronchitis.

How fortunate I was there, I thought. I suffered for decades from bronchitis, including four bouts of bronchial pneumonia with hospitalizations. No American doctor could cure me, and in 1993, when I was lecturing in Siberia, I spent as much time coughing as talking.

"Why are you coughing so much?" asked the regional minister of education who had invited me there to lecture to university administrators.

"Oh, I have bronchitis," I answered.

"Why do you still have bronchitis?" she asked. "You have been here four days already." Now that was a strange question.

"I have had bronchitis for 18 months," I explained, puzzling over her comment. "I have no cilia in my bronchi tubes because of many bouts of bronchial pneumonia, so colds turn immediately into bronchitis. I have it every year for many weeks."

"No, no, no," she remonstrated. "Bronchitis should not last more than three days. No one in Siberia has bronchitis for more than three days. So, American doctors don't know how to cure bronchitis? Our doctors do. You will go see our doctor when you finish your lecture."

True to her word, she led me, protesting in vain, to the doctor after the lecture ended. The doctor confirmed the diagnosis from the States: bronchitis.

"You must come to the clinic every day for three days," he told me. "After that, your bronchitis will be gone. Please don't skip a day; it is important that we clear up this condition."

Three days? Entirely skeptical and not one bit hopeful for any amelioration of my condition, I dutifully followed the doctor into the respiratory therapy room. There he turned me over to a nurse, who gave me a hand-held device that emitted a cold, thick vapor. *Ingalatsiya efkaliptom* (eucalyptus-based respiratory therapy) had been ordered for me. For 15 minutes, I slowly inhaled and exhaled the cold vapor and noticed that during the therapy session I did not feel any need to cough.

My cough, in a milder form, did return in a few hours. So, I returned the next day hopeful and no longer entirely skeptical. The nurse recognized me. "*Ingalatsiya efkaliptom*," she said, handing me the inhaler that I now knew how to use.

After 15 minutes, I returned the device to her, thanked her, and left, feeling no need to cough until the next day and then only once or twice. Amazing! I seemed to have licked the coughing. With one day of therapy left, after the morning lecture, which I got through without coughing even once—something I had not been able to do in 18 months—I headed off to see my respiratory therapy nurse with alacrity. I took the device and, convinced now of its merits, deeply breathed in the vapor for 15 minutes. Finished, I handed the device back to the nurse and left the clinic for the last time. That was in November 1993. I have never had bronchitis since. Certainly, I suffer from time to time from colds that would like to slide down past my cilia and develop into bronchitis, but, having learned the Siberians' secret, I pull out a bottle of eucalyptus oil and sniff it the minute I feel a cough coming on. Generally, it takes only 2-3 uses over a morning or an afternoon, and the bronchitis germs scamper off. I have given away my bottle of eucalyptus oil on many occasions. Each time, the recipient has related a story similar to mine: bronchitis gone in less than a day.

Once, I observed one of our secretaries taking antiobiotics upon her return from a two-week illness. "What are the antiobiotics for?" I asked her.

"Bronchitis," she said. "I have been fighting it for more than two weeks."

"No, no, no," I remonstrated, just like the Siberian minister of education 17 years earlier. "Bronchitis should not last more than three days." I handed her a bottle of eucalypytus oil, instructing her to sniff it whenever she felt a cough coming on. (Lacking the Siberian inhalation devices, sniffing is the closest I can come to emulating the Siberian natural cure. It works.)

Near the end of the day, I checked on the secretary. "How are you doing?"

"I have not coughed all afternoon," she said. "It's like this stuff cured me instantly. Amazing!"

So, after Mass on Sunday, I stood at the very end of the line so that I could share the Siberian remedy for bronchitis with the priest. "I don't come to your church," I told him. "I attend Mass in San Ignatio, but today I missed Mass there so decided to come here with my son." Doah shook the priest's hand.

"I think I was supposed to be here today," I explained, telling him my history and suggesting that he try eucalyptus oil. He thanked me and assured me that he would do so.

From his response, I was certain that he would test out the Siberian remedy (he did), and I could not imagine any result other than his bronchitis disappearing quickly (it did). I supposed he might think that I was some kind of angel sent his way—just once—to help with a just-once need for a cure to a troubling medical problem. Realizing that, I think I better understand where some kinds of angels may come from: God working through real people for a brief moment to execute a specific task on behalf of a particular person.

As I left the church, I thought of the irony: I came looking for an answer, and instead, I gave an answer to a priest in need. Then it hit me. Wham! That *was* my answer. Sometimes God's answers are too brilliant, too out-of-the-box, too perfect for my imperfect mind to recognize. I was looking for an answer to the question, do I prosecute or not? God re-framed the question for me. The problem was not about me. The problem was about the employee. I made the connection when I realized that my attendance at Mass was not for my good; it was for the good of the priest. There was my answer: stop looking at myself as the central player, at what I should do and what I was feeling. Look, instead, at the employee, what motivated him and what he was feeling. How much above our ways are God's ways and above our thinking is God's thinking, to quote Isaiah (*Isaiah* 55: 8-9)!

When I realized that, I knew what the next step had to be. I also knew I would, with God's help, be able to share God's grace and love with the employee when I next met with him.

As soon as I arrived at work, I said a prayer, then called the human resources officer. No answer. So I sent an e-note. Subject line: Occurrence of a felony in Division C. In the body of the message, I wrote: "If I have successfully gotten your attention, please call me." I had. She called me within minutes. I explained what had happened and what I wanted to do about it. She liked the approach.

After lunch, the human resources officer came to my office, read the contents of the documents the employee had given to my secretary, and confirmed that they contained nothing that could get me into any kind of trouble but might embarrass me. She took the documents for transferal to the Legal Office.

I had the employee's supervisor send him to me. I welcomed him as if nothing had happened, talked to him about a few routine matters, then asked him to sit down, silently praying for God to guide me through the conversation and help me to remember that this employee was every bit as much a child of God as I.

I pulled out the envelope with the condemning file. "Is this the envelope you gave to my secretary on Friday?" I asked. He confirmed that it was.

"Is this the negative 'documentation' that you told me you had on me?" I asked. Again, he confirmed that it was.

"Did you hope by means of this document to get me to change my position on your transfer?" I asked. He was quiet, unsure of how to answer, clearly worried about what lay behind this line of questioning. His eyes looked for a place to hide, but there was none. I was looking directly at him, and so was the human resources officer.

"Let me share with you my perception of this," I said and went on to talk about the seriousness of blackmail, informing him that I do not allow myself to be blackmailed, no matter what the nature of the documentation.

"You have put me in a very difficult position," I concluded. Then I showed him the legal definition of blackmail, which he could see for himself described what he had done. I also gave him a printout of the US and California penal codes that listed blackmail as a felony and the punishment as imprisonment and heavy fines. From his expression, I realized that he had not known that he was committing a felony.

"I would like to know why you did this," I said in a questioning tone, one that I hoped would come across as interested and caring, not accusatory. I was, indeed, interested in knowing his motivation, especially if my perception was not the actual motivation.

He melted and asked if he could talk to me privately. The human resources officer would not allow that, interjecting, "It is too late for that. The minute I leave this office, this becomes an official investigation, and she may not discuss this with you again. If you have something to say, you need to say it now."

He hesitated, then broke down. He had felt singled out by the transfer. Something I had said during the meeting had made him feel that I did not respect him. Most important, the document he had given me, in his opinion, showed that I had favored the employee with whom I had corresponded. He felt that was unfair. With the human resources officer concurring with my sharing the information and confirming what I said, I told him that the employee he considered favored had received one of the lowest ratings in the division and more disciplinary actions than anyone else, which is the reason he had left the division four years earlier.

There was one more question in my mind. "You accidentally found this file four years ago," I said to the employee. "Clearly, you have kept it for four years. Why? Do you really mistrust me so much that you felt the need to save something that might some day help you defend yourself?"

"No," the employee responded quietly, and then astonished me with his answer. "I was not looking to defend myself. I was not looking to make you do anything at all. Or to stop you from doing something. My feelings were hurt. You did not care enough about me to let me stay here in this department that I love, where my heart is, and, from what I could read in this file, I really did believe that you liked this other employee much more than me. I gave you the document to get you to think about whether you were really being fair."

The human resources officer stepped in at that point and iterated that every employee in the division who could not travel had been reassigned. Everyone was being treated the same. It was surely something that the employee needed to hear. What he wanted to hear, I was certain, was something else.

"I know your heart is here," I affirmed. "Unfortunately, your body has to be somewhere else. Both you and I know that your health will not permit you to travel. If I put you on a plane, I could be killing you." He admitted that I was right on both counts.

At the end, we agreed that he would accept the transfer. We also agreed that he would erase the file from his computer. We shook hands on it. He told me as well that he had made only the one printout that he had given me. I told him that I believed him, and that since we had shaken hands, I accepted his word as evidence that the problem was resolved and the file would be erased, that I had no intention of double-checking or of investigating further. At that point, the human resources officer returned the envelope to me, and both she and the employee left, in different directions.

I am confident that the matter is resolved. The employee is a Middle Easterner, and Middle Easterners prize being known as honoring their word. Moreover, he became truly frightened when he learned the punishment for blackmail. The fear that oozed out of him enveloped me, and in response an immense sense of compassion welled up inside and flooded me, spilling over onto him to wash away his fear. I experienced it as a unique God-driven phenomenon. That is what happens when I invite God to my counseling sessions and allow God to lead me through them.

In the days that followed, the employee came to me on several occasions for help as his dreaded transfer drew near, and I found myself comforting him upon each of these occasions. At his farewell lunch, I gave him a gentle hug that he seemed to need and told him to stay in touch. He promised to do so.

I am thankful that this situation had a happy ending. I am grateful to God for once again spoiling me and taking care of my problem. I am also grateful for the lesson learned: arrogance got me into the mess, humility got me out of it. If I can just remember to stick with humility only, I just might avoid most such messes in the future.

Leave Cancelled

A second example does not reflect well on my leadership. Fortunately, God, as usual, got the last word.

A devout senior manager had taken annual leave this past Christmas. I had approved the leave. I expected a quiet two weeks. However, the morning of Christmas Eve, I had an inquiry about a task in that manager's section that, it turns out, had not been completed. That task was urgent, visibly so. In fact, the visibility of the matter extended all the way to our Washington, D. C. headquarters. I checked with the junior manager, a new appointee. Not only had she done nothing; she was unwilling to do anything. Her supervisory chain and I had earlier come to the difficult conclusion that she did not have the skills for the position and was not trainable. So, we had decided that once we had a replacement, we would demote her.

Pushed to get the results to Washington immediately, faced with a junior manager unwilling or unable to accomplish this, lacking the necessary information to do the task myself, and angry that the senior manager had left everything locked up and out of reach, I called the latter at home and insisted that he come in. He did not want to do this—he had company—but he is a team player and dedicated, so in he came.

My mood not being conducive to polite interchange, for the rest of the day I steered clear of him and another junior manager he had pulled into the task to help. They both worked into the evening of Christmas Eve, as did I, awaiting their results. As I told my confessor later, I simply wanted my anger and could not seem to let go of it. I thought that I had hidden it by hiding myself from the two managers, but both later told me that I do not hide emotions well!

Late evening, I pushed the button that sent everything to the Washington office. It would be awaiting those in charge the minute they arrived at work on December 26, the equivalent to having had it to them at the end of their day on December 24.

That night, exhausted, I nonetheless made it to midnight Mass. My anger did not follow me to Mass, so I could relax and enjoy a refreshing end to a difficult day.

After Mass, I would normally have fallen into bed but I was overcome by a strong urge to read my email. At 1:30 in the morning?! I opened the email; there was only one note. It was from the senior manager. He related to me how distressed he was from having been called in from leave and being treated like he was a bad employee when he was both competent and loyal (he is). He was so upset, he said, that he could not bring himself to attend midnight Mass.

"Go to Christmas Mass tomorrow," I wrote to him, feeling immensely guilty but not knowing how I could otherwise have handled the work crisis that was caused in great part by his own delays—I suppose the not knowing how else to handle things could have been a result of my not having asked God to begin with. "That is an order. God can put right what man (or woman) has made wrong." Then I went to bed.

The senior manager sent me another e-note later on Christmas day. He had gone to Christmas Mass and had found peace there. Amen!

The Extra Manager at an EEO Meeting

A couple of years ago, two of my senior managers and I were called by our Equal Employment Opportunity (EEO) office to a pre-mediation discussion with our organization's attorney and human resource director. The complaint, filed by an older employee from one of our branch offices, was discrimination based on age. His first-line supervisor, Shirley, had fired him for absenteeism and poor performance. Prior to this meeting, I had, as usual with such meetings, asked God for guidance. (I don't like to make decisions that affect people's lives without God's assistance.)

Once assembled, we introduced ourselves and our role at the meeting. The role of most was clear. Roger was Shirley's supervisor, and I was Roger's supervisor. However, why Marvin had been called in was a puzzle to everyone, including to the EEO specialist, who did not remember inviting Marvin. Marvin was not in the complainant's supervisory chain. We all agreed that it looked like an accident that Marvin was there but he stayed because he had come in the same car with Roger and me and would be stranded until we were ready to leave.

It appeared that Shirley had done an adequate job of counseling the employee and had some documentation to back up the firing. Curiously, the employee had only asked for reinstatement for six months as redress. I moved the discussion away from whether we could give a non-discriminatory reason for the firing (we could) and whether we could back that up with documentation (we could) to why the employee would ask only for a six-month reinstatement. It turned out that this was the amount of time left that he needed to work in the organization in order to retire. Having started with us pretty late in life, he was already of retirement age and would be unable to find another job where he could work long enough to qualify for retirement benefits. Based on this information, I ventured that we not look at this complaint as one in which we could justify whether we had done things right (followed all the rules) but rather as one in which we could justify whether we had done the right thing (the humane approach to a person's life).

Shirley could not retain the employee long enough for him to be able to retire. There seemed to be no choice except to cut the cord in advance of retirement, and our lawyer began moving in that direction. At that moment, Marvin spoke up. He is the senior manager of a set of projects, one for which the employee could work on a flexi-place, short-term basis. Marvin suggested that he could assign the empoyee six months of work on a special project and stated that he would be willing to take him on. Voila! A chance to the right thing!

"Now I think we all know why you were called to this meeting!" I told Marvin.

The Grace of a Lost Wallet

As I was returning from a routine business trip to our Washingotn office, I reached into my purse for my wallet to pay the cab driver who had just pulled up in front of Dulles International Airport. I searched, and I searched again. The wallet is large. It could not hide. It was definitely gone, lost, but not likely purloined. I figured I had dropped/ or left it somewhere. I paid with the business credit card.

After entering the airport, I sat down and zipped off a note to one of the employees in our Washington office. Perhaps the wallet had fallen out there. I would have to await her response overnight because by the time I had made it to the airport, she had left for the day.

While I waited, all kinds of scenarios popped into my mind. Who might find the wallet, and what might he/she/they do with it? It contained sixty dollars in emergency cash I had taken as an advance on my credit card for traveling. I would have to repay it, but at least my *per diem* would cover it. Fortunately, too, my wallet contained no credit cards. It did have some stamps from by-gone years; none that would send a letter anywhere this year. It also had some of my business cards so anyone who found it would know where to send it! It would be interesting to see if I got it back. With the money? Without the money?

One happy scenario had a kindly and honest person finding it and, seeing the business cards, dropping the wallet into the mail to me, money and all. Or, without the money.

Another happy scenario had an honest person calling me or writing me at the coordinates on my business card and letting me offer to pay for the mailing of the wallet and/or letting me offer an award.

Another scenario, sadly, had a person finding it, taking the money, and throwing the wallet away. Hm, what might that person do with the money? Give it to someone who needed it? Use it because he or she was desperate for money for his/her family and saw the wallet as an unrequested gift? Or, using it, and years later, having not returned it, deciding that since the money could not be returned, passing on the same amount to another person—any person anywhere in need. I wanted to think that the money might help someone.

I knew, though, that the wallet might just as likely be found by a reprobate, who would take the money without a twinge of conscience and use it to buy booze or something else equally unhealthy. Sigh! My first reaction was, "Well, s/he will get his or her comeuppance when everything is over and done with. God will make sure that this person gets punished for his/her dishonesty."

But wait, what if that person were to repent at some point for all his/her acts of dishonesty. Then, there would no punishment. The grace of God forgives completely—even the expenditure of my money by someone else. So, I would lose the money, and someone else would gain it unfairly, and ultimately, would be washed clean of any wrong doing by the grace of God!?? Now, was this fair? Was I supposed to *like* this scenario?

Oh, yes, I did like even this scenario. After all, I had needed the grace of God; still do. So, if the choice was between getting my money back and having someone receive the grace of God, was there really any need to think about a preference? Oh, I did believe in the grace of a lost wallet!

I never asked God for any help with that wallet. I just went on with my life and figured it would find its way home or not. I did, however, pray about something else. Earlier in the day, I had taken a Super Shuttle ride from Dulles Airport to our Washington office. The driver was a friendly guy. When he found out that I did not have a ticket and the shuttle was going to leave in a few minutes, he personally walked me through the convoluted path to the ticket counter and back. Nice guy. Arab, I believed. It took nearly an hour to reach my office in the rush hour traffic, during which I added to the five hours of sleep I had just gathered on the red-eye from California, dozing during most of the trip. I had no luggage, and I was the first person off the shuttle. So, I hopped off, with a thank you to the driver, who graciously wished me a good day.

As I entered the building, it slowly dawned on me that Super Shuttle is a taxi and not a company-supplied van, which I usually take but could not this time because the trip had come at short notice. I should have tipped the driver. I headed back out the door, just as the driver re-started the van and pulled out of the driveway. Feeling that I had been stingy, I asked God to take care of the driver that day and see to it that he got good tips. I felt confident that as a result of that prayer the driver would indeed have a good-tip day.

When I arrived home from this trip, the response to my note to our Washington office was waiting for me. The person I contacted had looked everywhere but had seen no wallet. So, all those other options as to who might find it and what he or she might do remained open.

I did not have to wait long. During a morning meeting, my phone rang. I glanced at the number: an unknown 240 number. So, I let voice mail take the call. After the meeting, I called voice mail. There was a man, who called himself Amr, speaking with a distinctively Arabic accent, saying that I had dropped my wallet in the Super Shuttle van. He had been the driver (whom I had not tipped). He wanted to return the wallet to me and asked for me to return his call.

I was about to return Amr's call when the phone rang again. This time it was Amr's supervisor, who was a native speaker of English. He had given the wallet to her and asked her to call because he thought perhaps I was not able to understand Arabic-accented English. (Little did he know how much time I have spent with people who speak Arabic-accented English!) The supervisor told me that my checkbook was in there (I had forgotten about that), along with my business cards, stamps, and

$56 in cash. Yep, that is exactly as it should have been. She offered to fedex the wallet to me. I told her to use some of the cash for mailing fees and give the remainder of the money to Amr. She was surprised and said that Amr did not expect a reward but would obviously be pleased.

So, God did answer my prayer. Amr did have a good-tip day. As with so many of my answered prayers, I could not have predicted the outcome that I, the one who had not tipped him, would ultimately be the one to provide the good-tip day for Amr. Moreover, it was not even an expenditure for me because my *per diem* would be double that. I had taken about half of my *per diem* from an ATM just to have some money for meals. However, because I was all day with the CEO, my office provided all the meals, and I had been allowed to keep the *per diem*. So, Amr made nearly $50 on a tip, and I made nearly $50 on *per diem* post-tip. Win-win. I could never have planned that, let alone even thought of an outcome of this nature. I have reached the conclusion that I don't ever want God to answer my prayers in my way because God's ways are always so much better than the ways I can dream up! I just love watching the many unique ways, in which God sprinkles grace onto all!

VIP or VOP?

As someone who tries to follow the practices of St. Francis, I try not to overaccumulate possessions and to share with others, in keeping with Jesus's advice to the leader who wanted to get to Heaven to sell everything he owned, distribute it to the poor, and then come and follow Him (*Luke* 18: 18-23). In 2000, Donnie and I gave away nearly all of our possessions, when we moved from a large house into an RV for a number of years. I have never felt a need for a collection of *things*. In fact, a colleague once said of me, "Most people collect objects; Beth collects people."

I have no fear of real poverty. I know that God will provide. Raised on a farm by a housewife with no income and a father who made $5,000 a year for a family of eight children. I attended the university on full scholarship, then worked my way through graduate school on teaching fellowships, and, ultimately, completed my doctorate in Moscow, thanks to the Russian government allowing me to finish free.

Integrating the spiritual and the secular in my life has been a challenge. My position as a senior leader in my organization sometimes requires a bit of flashiness—or at least, so it seems. So, how does a VIP (Very Important Person) take a VOP (Vow of Poverty)? This troubling non-equation can, at times, plague me. Take our annual formal ball, for example. The required attire is tuxedos for men and gowns for women. Now, being a VIP in our organization (by position, not necessarily by self-view) meant that I could not avoid attending the ball, and indeed my VIP-ness evidenced itself several times throughout the evening by what I was called upon to do and where I was required to sit. That is the work side of me.

The spiritual side of me is quite different. Usually that different spiritual side, with God's help and guidance, splashes out around me at work. Following St. Francis's model, I tend to give away what I have and make do with what remains although I do not experience the level of poverty to which St. Francis and his followers reduced themeslves but rather something more symbolic: frugality so as to share on a wider scale the fruits of one's work. I do not feel compelled to live this way; I feel impelled to do so. It brings me great happiness to use my fairly decent salary (albeit less than it might be if difficulties did not descend upon our family like snowflakes on Alaskan mountains on a winter day) to help those who have no salary at all, to pay off God's credit card, and to contribute to divine projects. Splurging on a fancy ball gown that I would wear only once, then, did not fit with my spartan lifestyle. I did not want to buy a gown; I wanted the gown money to help my kids with their medical bills, the orphans of Kaluga or Liberia with finding care and perhaps even homes, the children of Palomar with getting a school, and the strangers passing through my life in need of food. I find far more pleasure in helping them than in looking at a pretty dress. But this was a ball! And it was for my office where I was supposed to be some kind of role model!

I did have an alternative—or so I thought. Since our foreign nationals were allowed, indeed encouraged, to wear their national dress, I figured that perhaps the Arabs would allow me to claim their ethnicity for a night since I had lived in Jordan for more than two years as a resident. So, I donned a Jordanian *dishdasha* and, like Cinderella, left for the ball.

Yes, like Cinderella. Except for one thing—no ball gown! The closer I approached the ball on my 45-minute drive there, the more concerned I became that I would be sitting near the head table where everyone would have on their fancy tuxes and gorgeous gowns, and there I would be in a pretty but everyday dress that I had picked up for $7.50 (yes, the period is in the right place) on the streets of Aqaba from a shopkeeper whose wife had probably done the hand embroidery. I started to squirm, well, at least, emotionally. What would people think? If I were sitting with the rank-and-file, it would be one thing, but next to the head table in a dress that even the poorest of people in the Middle East could afford and would typically wear? What was I thinking? I could have afforded to buy a beautiful gown to show off for my employees and superiors. How dumb to have put my last dollar for this month in the church collection plate for this week's cause! If people who worked for me deserved to look pretty, so did I!

I was still squirming when I reached the ballroom. I should not have been. All my Arab national employees flocked to me, pleased as punch that I would dress as one of them. They wanted my picture taken with them. With ethnic pride, they introduced me to friends who had come with them. Oher nationalities suggested that next time it was their turn to be so honored, that I should don their native attire. (I think I will—I have some dresses from Russia, Uzbekistan, Brazil, and Turkmenistan in my closet, all of them gifts from friends and colleagues with whom I worked in those countries.) Needless to say, I enjoyed my gownless ball experience very much.

Driving home, I realized that my thoughts during the earlier drive to the ball had dramatically illustrated those of the leader in *Luke 18* who asked Jesus what it would take to get to Heaven. I was on the wrong side of that equation on my way to the ball. And how about that camel that could make it through an eye of a needle easier than a rich man can make it to Heaven? Well, thank God, I am not rich! But I was acting like it on the way in. Really, who cares what others think about what I am wearing physically? Is it not more important what I am wearing spiritually? Is not the armor of God far preferable to a pretty ball gown? I may have questioned that on the way *to* the ball but certainly not on the way *from* the ball.

God gives me everything I need. If I had needed a ball gown, God would have given me one. Instead, God showed me that my simple Jordanian dress was sufficient, just as God's grace is sufficient. So, any dollars I have, extra or not, belong to God. Deep down, I think I knew that on the way *to* the ball, too. Just sometimes, God has to reach down and clunk me on the head again.

Prayers for Tareq

Answers to prayers have come readily to our division. One of the most remarkable was the case of Tareq, who approached me to tell me that he needed to take some sick days in order to have a quadruple by-pass.

Tareq was an elderly man, a refugee from the Kurdish area of Iraq. He had been working in our division less than a year. So, of course, he was worried about his health benefits and his employment status. I assured him that I would keep his position open for him and that he should go have his surgery without worrying about anything at the office.

Surprisingly, Tareq returned to work the next day. I ran into him in the corridor in the afternoon. "What happened?" I asked him.

"They cannot do the bypass because they found cancerous growths. I need to go through chemotherapy to shrink the size of the tumors before they will be able to operate on my heart."

I wished him well and offered to do whatever I could to help. I suggested that he take some time off from work, but he preferred to come into work to take his mind off the nauseating effects of the chemotherapy. Except for the mornings on which he received his treatments, he never missed any work until the day arrived for his bypass surgery. The chemotherapy had successfully reduced the size of the tumors, but the cancer and overstressed heart combination bode ill for him. The doctor gave him a 3% chance of recovering sufficiently to return to work.

Tareq resigned himself to the day prior to surgery being his last day at work ever. On that last day, he said good-bye to all his colleagues. Then, he came to see me. I was out. I went to see him. He was out. He came back. I was again out. At that point, he had to leave for the hospital. So, he wrote me a short e-note. All it said was "please pray for me."

I forwarded that note to all the employees in our division. Although we have a strict rule, prohibiting bringing religion into the work place, I felt compelled to share Tareq's quiet plea. "If you have a belief system that will let you honor Tareq's request, please do so," I wrote in the introduction to the forwarded note.

Personally, I prayed that God would take care of Tareq. I did not pray for a specific outcome because I had no idea what would be best for him. Only God knew that. Since asking God to heal Janet's illness during the pre-conversion time that I was challenging God, I think about prayer differently. A focus on God's will, not on my desire for specific outcomes, dominates my prayers. I simply place the person in God's hands because I know that God can come up with a better solution than I can.

Each employee in our division approached Tareq's request in his or her own way. Some lit candles. Others said prayers. Jews, Muslims, Christians, and others rallied around Tareq as a cohesive group with one concern: Tareq's welfare. We sent flowers and cards. We also sent a representative, a colleague who was a personal friend of Tareq's.

Some weeks later as I was walking past Tareq's empty desk, I did a double-take. A smiling Tareq was sitting there. "When did you get back?" I asked in amazement.

"Today," he replied. "I beat the odds! My doctor is in shock!"

It was soon after Tareq returned to his desk that I realized how successfully God had used me to build a spiritual workplace. Others have noticed, too. When prayer requests come in, I send them out to all employees with the same note that I used for Tareq: "if you have a belief system that will allow you to honor this request, please do so." Recently, I attended a project presentation made by one of our employees to a group of clients. In his acknowledgments, he thanked me and others for our support. He also thanked God. After work one day, I came across a Jew and a Muslim, still in the office, discussing their prayer traditions or, in their words, "sharing a cultural moment." Cultural moments are fine in our organization; religious moments are not. For some reason, I ended up telling a piece of Zhenya's story to our CEO, calling it a miracle. He looked me straight in the eye and enunciated clearly, "No, you are the miracle."

Indeed, I am not the miracle. I am simply the instrument. I pray for guidance daily. I ask not to hurt anyone and if possible to help someone during the day. People come to my office after work to pray, or if they are not Christian, to talk about prayer, their religious beliefs, or their spiritual needs. If they need a prayer rug, I have one.

God has blessed me with these wondrous opportunities to see how divine love can permeate an organization.

Through God's intercession, our division has become a living, vibrant organism. People are palpably excited to come to work. They support each other. They pray for each other. They ask for help if they need it. They give help where they can. Yes, we have farther to go. I noticed this recently in conducting a management training session, where some of the middle managers told me that it is difficult for them to like everyone and that they think all is well as long as they treat all employees equally, fairly, and with respect. Well, no. One senior manager pointed out that people know when others are "faking" positive attitudes toward them, that it is important to like every employee genuinely, including the so-called "difficult" ones, who become far less difficult if they know they are liked. Little do most of them know that I plan to push them not into liking everyone but into loving everyone. With God's help, they will learn. We all will learn. God's lessons and love are nonpareil.

Along the Path

As I became more comfortable with a drastically revised understanding of the universe, I began to traverse the path God laid out before me. There are, of course, moments when I get stuck at whatever hollow I am in. For example, from time to time I still get into arguments where I think arguments are warranted. God has not turned me into a namby pamby person. I never have been namby pamby. I don't know how to be namby pamby. As a mother of two handicapped children (three, if you count Shura) and grandparent of two children with serious medical issues, I could not afford to take a back seat, accepting whatever I was told. Had I done that, my handicapped children would have died. I have had to argue with doctors where it was clear that they were wrong—and standing my ground, with Donnie's support, of course, did indeed save my children's lives more than once.

Perhaps God does not mean for us to change who we are but what path we follow. In that respect, I have far to go, especially taking the word, *follow*, as the operant one. In my career, I have always been a strong leader. Is it possible for me to become a humble follower?

God's People

I do not walk the path alone. In the difficult moments or those moments when I am straying, God often sends me help in the form of other people who can nudge (or push) me back onto the path—a beloved priest or nun, an in-tune friend, a stranger; the list is varied. God seems able to use just about anyone when needed. On more than one occasion God has used Jean. Other times God has sent me lessons, reminding me that all people are God's people.

The Letter

I once wrote a rather nasty note to an interim priest. He said something negative about our previous parish priest during Mass, in the presence of that priest, something that was not true and clearly hurt our former priest's feelings. It was an attempt by the interim priest to make a joke, but it fell flat. The inappropriateness of it stirred feelings of indignation within me. (There we go with judgment! Who am I to judge? Yet I did!)

I decided to write an irate letter, something that is generally out of character for me when it comes to priests. I highly value all the priests in my life and am grateful for them and to them, and I certainly do not expect them to be perfect. In this case, though, I was certain that I had the high road, and I explained all my concerns to the interim priest in *four* written pages!

As I folded the letter to mail it, I felt a twinge out of nowhere, a strong feeling that what I was doing was wrong. However, being in a happily judgmental mood, I started to seal the envelope. The twinge came again. Okay, I considered, so maybe this twinge means that God does not want me to send this letter. I thought it over, figured I knew better than God, and, still in my great judgmental mode, rewrote the letter, removing all the vitriol and about half the contents. I then sealed the envelope and busied myself with something else.

As I busied myself, that twinge came yet again. Stronger this time. Oh, for heaven's sake, I thought, I better rewrite the thing again. So, I threw away the envelope with the original letter and revised what I had written. When I was done, the letter was only one page and, I thought, pretty kindly and succinctly worded. The revised note went into an envelope, which I sealed, stamped, and put into my purse for mailing during my lunch hour the next day.

When I reached my office the next morning, I was surprised to find Jean waiting for me. She was supposed to be at a conference.

"I am leaving right now," she said, "but I am supposed to tell you something. I have no idea what I am talking about. So, I am just going to say it straight out, and perhaps you can figure out what is meant. You should not mail the letter you have written because the person to whom you have written it is too weak."

Jean has had this sort of thing happen to her more than once, but, as usual, she had no more insight than she had already given me. When I told her that the only letter I had written was to our interim priest, she was surprised but nonetheless certain that I was not supposed to mail it. I promised to consider her words, and she left.

I took out the letter, read it again, and decided that, just in case, I should rewrite it one more time. I cut it down to one very gentle paragraph and put it in a new envelope. (I am an obstinate one; no wonder God had to conk me on the head to get me to convert and even now occasionally has to get a little rough with me.)

At that moment, the phone rang. It was the interim priest. He asked me to go to the Holy Thursday Chrism Mass, where the bishop blesses the oils for use at Easter and distributes them to representatives from each parish in the diocese. He wanted me to join the two other parish representatives and pick up the Oil of Catechumens (used in baptism, blessing of altars, and consecration of churches), Holy Chrism (used in confirmation, baptism, and consecration), and Oil of the Sick (used in unction, i.e. annointing the ill) for our parish. He would not be there.

"Why not?" Being curious, I let the question escape unchecked.

He was evasive. "I have to go to San Francisco."

"Well, can't you go on a different day?"

"No, I have to go that day."

"Why?" As I said, I can be pushy and curious.

"I have a doctor's appointment."

"Is something wrong?" I was not about to let him evade my questions, and I was definitely getting a sense of something being indeed seriously wrong.

"Well, I may need some surgery, or at least, an opinion on whether to medicate or to operate." I know he did not really want to give me this information, but he did not know how to evade my instinct, honed from raising many children, for pinpointing problems and my well developed tenacity in worming information out of the recalcitrant.

"What kind of surgery? What's wrong, Father?" Something told me that he needed to tell someone what was happening.

I believe I was right because he yielded and told me that he was battling cancer.

"Father, you should share this with the parish," I said. When he said it was personal and therefore private, I countered, "People love you. They are going to want to support you, to help you, to pray for you. You need to let them do that."

I tore up the letter as we spoke. At our next Mass, he shared the fact that he would, indeed, be having surgery. The parishioners rallied around him.

I also led a prayer vigil for him. Then, on the day after his successful surgery, I drove to the distant city and took him flowers from the parish and the candle we had used for the vigil, which I had placed during our prayers in a candle holder that I had brought to the USA from my days of living in the Holy Land.

So, God got my attention, and I finally listened to what God wanted. The bottom line, though, beyond the lesson to "judge not," is that when God says "no," God means no. God's will always wins, at least in my life, and that is as it should be.

Airport Companions

In April 2010, God taught me yet another lesson. At that time, the Eyjafjalla-jokull volvano in Iceland erupted, making travel to and through Europe difficult: long lines, canceled flights, re-routed planes. It was a good time to curtail one's travel, but I could not do that. Neither could many other people, and so at airports one found impatience and irritation rampant.

I quickly encountered these emotions myself. Well, honestly speaking, I fell captive to them when the first leg of a series of flights I was scheduled on was re-routed after we had already boarded. Everyone had to be rescheduled. Most of us were making connections that we would miss, so the line was long and slow, a couple of hours slow.

A Vietnamese couple several people behind me kept pushing, trying to get ahead of those in front of them. How not American, I thought, determined to make them take their turn in accordance with my American sense of proper behavior.

There were three of them: the elderly couple and a young woman, whom I assumed to be their granddaughter. They chatted away in an Asian language that I did not recognize but later learned was Vietnamese.

As they pushed forward, the elderly man elbowed me aside, trying to slide around me as the line began to inch around the twists and turns leading to the ticket counter. I had watched him use this maneuver to leapfrog successfully in front of about a dozen people, one at a time. Now I separated him from his wife and the young woman, and, having stood in line for close to 90 minutes already, knowing that each passing minute lowered the chances of finding a flight that would allow me to connect to my other legs, I was decidedly impatient with the process and irritated with someone who felt he deserved to go first. (Of course, I did realize that this was simply his culture; he probably had no idea how Americans, who are raised to take turns, are annoyed by what would be a normal jockeying for position in his own land.) Having spent time in countries where one must jockey for position or never make it to the counter, I knew how to hold my own place and did, continuing to separate him from the two who were with him.

Feeling uncomfortable about the whole situation, I did what extroverts always do. I struck up a conversation. The elderly couple did not speak English. However, Twi, the young woman, who, it turns out was not their granddaughter but just another line-stander, did speak English, albeit almost unintelligibly. She spoke to the couple in Vietnamese and to me in bad English, and slowly a picture of each other emerged.

The elderly couple stopped pushing. The four of us were now a group and could proceed through the line together until we were separated into two groups at the ticket counter. The elderly couple took the first open ticket agent. Twi, who had asked me to interpret for her, and I took the second. It is not the first time that someone whose language I do not speak has asked me to interpret. You see, if you work with foreigners frequently, you learn how to speak broken English in a way that they can understand when they cannot understand grammatically correct and rapidly spoken English. You also learn how to understand what they are trying to say when they know only 1-2 words out of the dozen that they need. So, I interpreted for Twi and successfully arranged her new flight for late afternoon. Since she would have a 6-hour wait, she called her husband to meet for lunch. He would meet her at the baggage claim, where all our bags had been sent.

I had to go pick up my bag, as well, because my new flight was leaving from another terminal. San Jose Airport is easy to navigate, but Twi was new both to the airport and to the English language, so I offered to walk her over to the baggage claim area and get her on the right curb to meet her husband. After that, I could catch the bus to the other terminal.

As we left the ticket counter, I saw the elderly couple standing by, looking confused. They had just received their new tickets but clearly had not understood anything about what their next step should be. I looked at their tickets; they were on my flight. Twi explained to them that they would have to get their luggage and take a bus to the other terminal. They panicked until they understood that I was on their flight and would accompany them the whole way.

Having crossed the overpass, obtained our luggage, and dropped Twi at the right curb, the couple and I were ready to clamber on the shuttle bus. I stepped up first and threw my bag onto the shelving. Then, I noticed the elderly, stereotypically small, Asian man struggling to lift two large bags. Equally small but a farm-raised girl with eight years of military duty under my belt, today I can lift and swing heavy suitcases much the same way as I used to lift and swing bales of hay. I hopped back out, grabbed the two suitcases and swung them onto the rack.

We stayed together, minimally communicating, given the lack of a common language, until flight time. They got off first in Phoenix, my first layover and an airport I know well. They were muddling through an interpretation of the airport signs when I disembarked and was rewarded with a second chance to help them.

I understand the lesson God wanted me to learn that day: be kind, be helpful, give up irritation and impatience. In the process, I was given a chance to become acquainted with two people who otherwise would have been only faces in a crowd. How interesting that once we know someone, our attitude dramatically changes for the better. As for them, they were very grateful. "Thank you" was the one American expression they did know, and they used it over and over. In spite of the aggravation of disrupted travel, I arrived cheerful, thanks to two people I did not know and whose language I did not speak.

Now, when faced with long lines at the airport, as happens more frequently than not, I try to remember this lesson. I have often been the recipient of the kindness of strangers when I travel. I like it when the shoe is on the other foot, when I can be the stranger who shows kindness. At the end of the day, we are all God's children; we should work together and play together in ways that demonstrate we know this.

Mercy

Noelle's significant other of ten years, Ray, passed away earlier this year at the end of a short and difficult life. Noelle and Ray were unlikely partners. Noelle was the product of an educated Caucasian family from the East Coast, and Ray was the product of a Black minority community on the West Coast. What they shared was physical disability, attacks on their health, and a deep, inseparable love.

Born with spina bifida like Noelle, Ray had spent the last four years battling intermittent kidney failure, in and out of a coma, and on and off respirators at one hospital or another. He was undergoing dialysis when he suffered a stroke and heart attack that rendered him once more comatose. His brain showed no activity for a full week, and the hospital ethics committee ruled that he should be taken off the respirator. Noelle was to go to the hospital at 6:00 that evening and be present when Ray's life support was shut down. I promised to pick her up right after work and take her there. This was something that Noelle did not want to do but knew she had to. At least, I would be with her.

At 9:20 a.m., Noelle called me at my office. "Mom, you're not going to believe what happened," she said. "You don't have to take me to the hospital tonight."

"Really? Why not?"

"The hospital just called. Ray's respirator hose broke, just like that. No one knows why. They told me that this never happens, and they are going to investigate. No one touched it. It just broke all by itself, and Ray died instantly."

"Goodness!" What else could I say?

"Mom, it is better this way. I am so relieved. I did not want to watch Ray die." While Noelle experienced much grief from losing Ray, there was immense relief in her voice.

"This is a blessing, Mom," she told. "A real blessing. He did not die by my hand. He just died because his life was over."

Sometimes God's kind mercy is so startling that one cannot even say a normal prayer but just keep repeating over and over in awe and gratitude, "My Lord and my God, thank You!"

Miracles of Healing

Thinking about the tender mercy we experienced in Ray's situation brings to mind miracles of healing that I have experienced myself. Sometimes I wonder if I get a disproportionate share of them, only two of which are described below, or have just learned to recognize them. Perhaps miracles of healing or any other sort happen more often than people realize. I wonder how many miracles we miss through inattention, let alone through disbelief. The signals are sometimes so slight that it is easy to miss them if we are not tuned in, don't pay close attention, or just dismiss the unusual as a curiosity. Sometimes, I wonder why God keeps sending them to us when we treat them so cavalierly.

Urine Infection

Documented evidence of medical anomalies, such as Ray's broken respirator hose, are easier for others to accept, I have found, than undocumented ones. There is a tendency not to believe anything that appears supernatural. So, what happened in the incident I relate here may be less believable to others, but I worked hard to create a small bit of personal evidence for myself. I, too, do not always want to believe a supernatural explanation for events. Sometimes, though, the evidence says that I must take more on faith than I am inclined to.

In August 2008, I was in a very rural area of Russia, hours from medical care, when I developed a urine infection. It became increasingly worse over 4-5 days, and on the fifth evening my bladder seemed to have shut down.

I collected a urine specimen because I knew doctors would need that, and the sample looked very infected. Having had a UTI before that had shut down my bladder and sent me to the emergency room, I knew the symptoms, and this one was bad. There was no option for local care. Regional care was not only hours away but also not available in the middle of the night. Even transportation would not be available until morning. I tried to fall asleep, but the pain was too severe for that. After two hours of tossing, turning, running to the bathroom in the hope that my bladder would start working again, and trying hard to ignore pain that kept increasing in intensity, I prayed for the strength to tolerate the pain until morning when I could seek help.

Suddenly, I was not alone. A male figure in a calf-length brown robe and sandals was with me. I could not see past the hem of his robe because when I saw the hem of the brown robe and the strong, masculine feet in Middle Eastern sandals, a great awe spread through me. I closed my eyes and was afraid to look up. The robed figure laid strong, large hands on my abdomen, and I felt warmth spread throughout my body. Nearly immediately I was asleep.

I awoke a few hours later, totally refreshed, and in no pain. Even my bladder was working. I collected another urine sample—perfectly clear.

Convinced that I must have been dreaming the infection and the figure in brown, I double-checked the urine sample from the evening before. It was clearly infected.

Rotator Cuff Injury

A second incident *has* been medically documented. I had fallen and injured the rotator cuff of my right arm, an injury that, I am told, rarely fully heals and often requires surgery. The local clinic took three x-rays, made the diagnosis, and sent me to a specialist in the city. The city doctor took two more x-rays, confirmed the diagnosis, and set me up for an MRI the following week.

Saturday evening I attended Mass with Doah. I often feel God's general presence at our mission church; many people do. However, this time, while kneeling, I felt a presence right beside me along with a brief touch on my right shoulder. I leaned over to Doah afterward and asked if he had just felt the same presence. He said he had. When we stood to say the Lord's Prayer, I noticed that for the first time in three weeks I felt no pain in my right arm. Then, during the sign of peace, I hugged a friend who was in the pew in front of me.

"Be careful of your arm," she warned me, knowing that I had not been able to lift it above waist level since the injury.

"It doesn't hurt," I told her, "and it is moving now."

Once I walked out of the church, I rotated my arm in all directions with ease and no pain. I then showed my full range of motion to a few friends who were with me. They were equally astonished.

In spite of my newly found mobility, I followed through with the MRI. No injury showed up on any of the scans. The orthopedic surgeon was spooked. I thought he might want to know what happened, but he did not. He offered no explanation and wanted none. He seemed eager to have me leave his office as soon as possible. Even though I am an extravert, I was unable to engage him in any conversation, and he had difficulty even looking me in the eye. I thought it a very odd reaction, but then, I suppose, he is not used to rotator cuff injuries simply disappearing.

This rotator cuff injury, the bladder infection, and other instances of healing have surprised me because I did not ask God to heal me at any of these times. (Of course, who does not *want* to be healed, whether or not one asks?) Essentially, God answered an unexpressed request. I guess this is why my Sufi friend tells me that God spoils me. God does. I don't ask why. I just say "thank you!"

On Being Worthy

I did not wake up in my usual manner one Sunday morning but rather to the barking of the alarm clock which I had set just in case I overslept. (I chose the sound of barking dogs because it sets my cats into motion—and *they* get me up.)

With the first cat bite on my toes from Intrepid and the simultaneous feel of Murjan's paw pulling the blanket off my face and tap-tap-tapping me on the cheek, I jumped out of bed, instantly realizing that I had missed the first Mass of the morning. I did want to catch the second since I had a noon BBQ with friends and would have no other options for Mass after that.

Donnie woke up at the same time, looked around groggily, and commented that I had fallen asleep before finishing the preparations for the BBQ. He could not do it all by himself; he would need my help before I left for Mass. My morning plans for contemplative prayer, followed by a perfunctory shower, followed by Mass, followed by a quick trip to the store for ice, followed immediately by the BBQ were instantly swapped out for a new set of plans: BBQ preparation and, sigh, laundry drying. By falling asleep early, I had not put the just-washed laundry into the dryer and had nothing to wear for the day.

At that point, I was wide awake. Let's see: no prayer, no shower, no clothes. What a way to start the day! I quickly found something marginally suitable in the closet to wear in lieu of attending Mass nude, threw the laundry into the dryer and the cats into the cat room where they would be out of the way and have a place to play, washed the kitchen floor, cleaning up the obvious signs of cats sharing our eating quarters, combed my hair which I would have preferred to wash, grabbed the keys, and ran to the car.

As I backed out of the driveway, I saw that I was already five minutes late for Mass. Fortunately, it is a 45-second drive to the mission (no walking today). I quickly parked, ran past the parish office, through the gardens, and into the church. The lector was reading. I had missed the blessing, sigh! (I like the blessing.) I had also missed any seating space. I looked and looked and finally saw a spot in the middle of one pew near the rear of the church. I asked the person on the end if I could slide in, and she moved over. Now I could relax.

I sat back to listen to the readings and then to the priest's homily, which was really, really good--everyone said so--but I had trouble concentrating. I knew the reading. It was about giving up earthly goods, which I have done three times in my life. I have never had many goods, anyway. Perhaps, therefore, I do not feel a need for such things. Or perhaps, as an Emersonian rugged individualist from Thoreau's New England, I do not want to be owned by my things. The priest began with narrating a monkey-trapping technique. When he started, the thought that ran through my mind was "and I need to know how to catch a monkey why?" Then it became clear that it was an analogy. The monkey does not let go of the food that has attracted it to a jar containing the food and into which an empty paw can enter but from which a full paw cannot withdraw. So, the monkey is trapped. We, too, are trapped when we won't let go of our earthly goods. It was food for thought, but my thoughts were elsewhere.

My thoughts centered on my irritation at waking up late, my plans going awry, having to finish the previous night's work, and, especially, missing my normal morning time in prayer with God. Seemingly, I had forgotten that I was at the moment sitting in a pew with my friends in the presence of God.

Fortunately, the sense of God's presence broke through in time for communion. Maybe not today, I thought. My mood makes me unworthy in spite of having mouthed the words, "Lord, I am not worthy to receive You, but only say the word and I shall be healed." I said themwithout listening--or perhaps did not believe that God would "say the word" today.

Having decided not to take communion (a first such decision for me), I contemplated whether to go down for a blessing or continue to nurse my irritation in the pew while others took communion. I decided that the pew was the best place for me, given my attitude and realizing that I had not actively participated in the Mass that I had so hurried to attend. "Sorry, God," I said silently, "I don't feel worthy to participate in the Eucharist this morning."

Wrong decision! I suddenly felt like I was being pulled into the aisle and pushed forward. I should have recognized all my ruminations as wrong thinking. I don't have to have done everything right to be worthy. I don't have to earn God's gifts. God showers us with grace and gifts freely. God wants our union. We are worthy simply because we are His. He *will* "say the word." He always does.

As I walked forward, I felt enveloped by pure Love, by God Himself. My irritation evaporated as I felt forgiveness and acceptance, remembering that worship is not about me but about God. God has demonstrated vast love for us from the conception of the human race, through centuries of our missteps and rebellion, and then later in those simple, powerful words of Jesus, "Forgive, them, Father, for they know not what they do."

Indeed, I often know not what I do, but I do know this: God forgives, God accepts, God graces. I therefore have the right neither to judge myself nor to hold myself apart from God. The choice is not mine. It is God's. It has always been God's, and God always wants me. Can anything else matter?

St. Bernard of Clairvaux talks about four stages of spiritual maturity: (1) loving ourselves for our own sakes, (2) loving God for our sakes, (3) loving God for God's sake, and (4) loving ourselves for God's sake. This lesson on worthiness has given me some insight into what it might mean to love myself for God's sake. It is a stage of development I have yet to reach, but I look forward to the time when God's grace will lead me there.

Enemies

My favorite movie of all time is *Enemies*. In it, two fighter pilots crash on a planet and are forced to work together to survive. They learn each other's languages and begin to understand each other's cultures. Their friendship becomes unbreakable. I can relate to that movie because most of my student and career years have been spent in the land of enemies: the Soviet Union, the Middle East, Central Asia, and, more recently, Afghanistan. I have learned their languages and their cultures. I have developed deep friendships. I have even adopted their children.

Thoughts of enemies arose again when at the end of one retreat, as we retreatants were sharing our peresonal concerns with each other, I told the group something about my pending assignment as part of a short consultation in a war zone. In so doing, I, described my worry that God just might want me to do the most dangerous part of the assignment and how I just might not *want* to follow God's will in this, depending upon what that turned out to be. I asked for their prayers.

In the weeks that followed, I had great difficulty discerning God's will for this assignment. Finally, I gave up trying to discern and did what I have done on other occasions when everything is cloudy. I asked God to close any door that I should not walk through because I fully planned to walk through any door that was open. As it turned out, when I reached the war zone, some doors were open, but the most dangerous one had been closed. The commanding general considered that particular mission too dangerous for a consultant at that paticular time.

Upon reflection, I realized that my request to the other retreatants for personal prayer was selfish There were four other groups involved in this assignment, not just me. We would all be together in one location. I would be involved only for a couple weeks; my colleagues would be involved for a year. I, however, not qualifying for weapons issue because of my civilian status, would be the only one with no protection except for the grace of God. (Oh, wait; there is no better protection than the grace of God!) The shameful part of my sharing is that I did not ask for prayers for all those others, including the enemies. I, who have lived in the lands of enemies off and on for 25 years forgot to ask for prayers for either my colleagues or my enemies! I, who have sat at tables with enemies and former enemies! I, who finished my doctorate, thanks to the help of enemies, i.e. the Russians, who allowed me to enroll at one of their universities and study there during and after the Cold War!

How small and mean is man, even that man who loves and tries to serve the Lord! No matter how we try, in a crisis we (with the exception of the saints and some extraordinary individuals who grace the pages of history) are merely ordinary people who put our own needs first. May God have mercy on us—and on our enemies!

I have since reconciled this weakness of mine with God, at least for now, for surely I will sin again. I have asked God to convert every selfish prayer to two prayers each for my enemies. Now, while I do make a concerted effort to pray for my enemies, I know that even if I forget, there will be prayers for them, anyway.

Ugly Roses

Walking through the Old Mission gardens after Mass one evening, I stopped to smell a breathtakingly beautiful rose. No smell. I thought no-smell roses only occurred in hothouses. Obviously, I thought wrong. So, I began to smell some of the other roses, and I noticed a very peculiar thing: the prettier the rose, the less the smell; the uglier the rose (misshapen, poorly fertilized, overrun by bugs), the sweeter the smell. Huh?! Who would have thought? I suppose if I were to ignore the "no huele/no cut" signs around the garden, I would have had a hard time choosing between a bouquet of visual beauty or one of sweet scent. I do believe, however, that I would have chosen the latter.

That brought to mind *Matthew* 19:30: "[In God's kingdom]. . . many who are first will be last, and many who are last will be first." "Superiors" have no priority over "underlings," nor do bosses pre-empt employees. The rich are not better than the poor. The pretty are not more attractive than the ugly, and the leaders of this world are not greater than the forgotten of this world. All the great achievements of this world make no difference in God's world where love and relationship trump money and possessions. Who we are inside trumps what we are on the outside, just as the inside of the flower (the scent) trumps the outside (the beauty).

Donnie and I spent the afternoon of the ugly-rose day with Doah, who in many ways resembles the sweet-smelling ugly roses. He is abnormally short (4'7") and stocky with a round face that cries out to be covered by a beard, which his group home will not allow him for reasons of hygiene. His mental development stopped somewhere around age 7, or more accurately, he developed very slowly, reaching age 7 in mental age about the time of his 21st birthday. People immediately notice that he is different, and sometimes those who do not know him go out of their way to avoid him. Those who know him, however, are fond of him and his giving nature.

Growing up, Doah never liked candy; he did not like the taste of sugar. However, he was the only one of my children who begged me to buy him candy, and his candy disappeared quickly. He never ate it. He shared one piece each with all of his friends, and he gathered a great many of them over time.

His behavior on the ugly-rose afternoon reminded me of his young days. Since he makes very little at the sheltered workshop where he works, I usually give him some money whenever I get together with him. That afternoon Donnie, he, and I had lunch together, and then I gave Doah $20 for the next couple of weeks. Doah begged us to stop off at CVS so that he could spend some of his money. There he purchased 48 cans of coke. I asked him with curiosity why he would spend $15 of his $20 on something that he cannot drink because of a medical problem with carbonated beverages. He explained that the 40-50 people who work with him at the sheltered workshop love soda, but none is available on site because it is too expensive; clients are restricted to water unless they bring drinks from home. Doah told us in the restricted language he uses, "I give; they happy."

I could have purchased the drinks for Doah rather than let him spend nearly all his money on his co-workers, but that would have mitigated the lesson he was teaching himself and spoiled his heart. He went home with $4.63 and a big smile that revealed an inner beauty that overpowered any abnormal physical appearance. I could almost catch the whiff of a rose.

If God Loves Me, Why Can't I Cook?

Everyone knows that I cannot cook a decent meal. As for the rest of my homemaking skills, let us just say that my passing grade in Home Economics as a child was a gift from a teacher who liked me but not necessarily a reflection of my homemaking ability. I think she just did not want to ruin my straight-A average. Maybe she gave me the grade for effort rather than result.

When my kids were growing up, if I wanted to get them to do something, I would just have to threaten to cook dinner myself rather than their dad. Even as youngsters, they knew how to cook well. (Their spouses love that.) As an adult, Doah wrote a book with my help, an exercise in understanding and developing literacy. The topic of all the tales in the book is my sad lack of homemaking skills and the horrendous outcome of my attempts to use them. The stories are as true as they are hilarious. Why I got missed in the distribution of talents that most women have, I may never know.

Every once in a while, though, I try to remedy the situation—to no avail. On Donnie's birthday recently, I decided to make him dinner, freeing him from that daily task. He protested, but then realized that this was going to be my gift to him so he let me try. I had purchased some fresh squid; they are easy to cook. A salad and some vegetables, rolls, desserts—voila! a great dinner! Except it was, following historic patterns, not edible. Donnie made himself a toasted cheese sandwich, and, as happens in such cases, I ate the inedible meal just to prove something. (Just what I am trying to prove in these cases, I am not sure.)

So, I ask, if God loves me, why can't I cook? This question parallels the kinds of questions that my catechism kids ask: if God loves me, why can't I do something I want to do, why don't I get an A grade on my project or test, why can't I have a specific gift or opportunity, i.e. why is life so tough sometimes? I love the book by Lorraine Peterson that attempts to answer this question: *If God Loves Me, Why Can't I Get My Locker Open?* I recommend it to all parents, catechists, and teenagers.

In thinking about this question, a possible answer begins forming in my mind. I cannot do things perfectly because I am human, ordinary. Not everything I want will go my way because it should not go my way. I need to walk in the path of the cross because that path that brings a different kind of life, one that leads to resurrection.

And then the life of Jesus comes to mind. He did not choose to live an extraordinary life but an ordinary one although the way he lived it was extraordinary. If he had not lived an ordinary life, we would not have the example of how we, as ordinary human beings, can and should live. He showed us how to live the way God would have us live, how to be servants to those around us, how to improve life for others, and how to bear our cross, whatever that may be, with grace and trust. He gave us the answer to the question that my catechism kids ask.

Why can't I get the locker open, cook a meal for my husband, have no financial worries, and birth only healthy children? I cannot do those things precisely because God *does* love me! Just like God loved Job. Just like God loved Jesus!

One Fine Lent

The season of Lent 2010 arrived at a time when I was following a strictly enforced, prescribed diet. No food items could be given up for Lent. However, I did find something I wanted to give up: frustration. Mounting frustrations from little things at work made me realize that I needed to eliminate frustration from my life, just as I had eliminated worry earlier (with rare exception do I ever worry about anything once it is in God's hands). After all, a wise priest once told me that frustration does not come from God but from the negative forces in life. I told fellow Catholics at work about my Lenten promise so that they could help by pointing out when I appeared to be becoming frustrated, and I prayed about it until the non-frustration habit began to be established as strongly as the non-worry habit.

Throughout Lent, there were many opportunities to test my progress. On an Alaskan Airlines flight from Seattle to San Francisco, for example, the gate agent would not let me carry on my backpack, claiming it was too big. Mind you, I had carried that bag on hundreds of flights across hundreds of thousands of air miles on nearly every American carrier and many foreign carriers over the past 4-5 years I had owned it. It was the perfect carry-on because it rolled when I didn't want anything on my back and had nicely padded straps for carrying when I needed my hands free. Had I not had both my computer and some breakable items in it, I would have cheerfully handed it over, but the reality was that I did have those things and the agent's insistence that the bag would not fit under the seat or in the overhead without confirming her supposition made me anything but cheerful.

Since the gate agent would not let me on the plane with the backpack, I pulled out the computer. put the breakables in a plastic bag I happened to have with me, handed the backpack to the agent, and, with an armful of loose goods, found my seat. Placing them on the floor, I grumpily sat down in my seat.

Once seated, I opened a wonderful book, but I could not get past the first few sentences without needing to go back and re-read. This happened several times before I realized I was frustrated. But I had given up frustration for Lent! That had lasted only four days? I dissolved into prayer, and the frustration dissolved!

The saga continued, however. Upon arrival in Seattle, my gate-checked bag was nowhere to be seen. I queried Mr. Wendell, the agent meeting the plane, about it. He asked for my orange tag. I did not have an orange tag. I had a white tag.

"Oh," Mr. Wendell said, "then you need to pick it up on the baggage carousal."

Clearly, that was not going to work. I was transferring from Alaskan Air to United Airlines. With Alaskan Airlines arriving a half-hour late and United being in a different terminal, where I still had to get my boarding pass, I had just barely enough time to grab the train between terminals, get my boarding pass from the ticket counter, clear security, and race to the departure gate. I explained this to Mr. Wendell, who asked for my claim tag, saying he would call and have the backpack transferred to the United flight.

Off I ran to the airport train, together with a senior manager from work, who had been traveling with me. I explained to him the situation with my backpack, noting in retrospect that I had told Mr. Wendell that I was taking the United flight but had not told him the flight number! Knowing of my decision to give up frustration for Lent, the senior manager commented, "But you're not frustrated, right?"

No, actually, I was not. I had put the opportunity to be frustrated in abeyance until I could talk to a United agent.

At the check-in counter, the ticket agent could not find any record of my bag. Since Mr. Wendell had my claim number, there was no way to search for it in the computer. She suggested talking to the baggage handlers planeside.

Off we ran again, frustration still in abeyance, clearing security quickly, thanks to our 1K frequent-flyer status. We dashed up to the gate on time. The plane was delayed. We would have to wait for an hour.

At least, that presented another chance to check on my backpack while there were still options, should it be sitting on the Alaskan Airlines baggage carousal rather than in the United cargo hold, pending transfer. I suggested that we wait in the Red Carpet Club. It was evening, and we had not eaten all day. The senior manager could snack on healthy munchies—carrots, celery, and fruit. I could check the status of my bag with the club's ticket agent.

At the club, the ticket agent could find no information in the computer. I had three options: (1) travel as planned, (2) stay in San Francisco and have Donnie pick me up there (a long drive), or (3) take the 10:00 flight (vice 7:30) and check the San Francisco carousal just in case.

The best choice was unclear. If Mr. Wendell had successfully transferred my bag, #2 and #3 meant that I would be in San Francisco and my bag at my final destination. If he had not been successful, #1 meant I would be home and my bag in San Francisco. Whether Mr. Wendell had been successful was a missing piece of critical information. Complicating matters was the fact that although I had taken out my computer and was carrying it with me, I had not taken out the power supply. (I made a mental note to myself: buy a spare power supply for traveling.) In addition, there was no identification on the backpack other than a handwoven purple strap from Korea with the letter B. (I made another mental note to myself: put identification labels on my carry-ons.) If the bag were to be left in San Francisco on the Alaskan Airlines carousal, no one would know to whom the bag belonged. Gate-side claim tags have no names, and the numbers are not entered into the computer. You are supposed to pick up the bag upon de-planing because it is traveling *with* you. Supposedly.

I called Donnie to tell him about the plane delay. He mentioned that he had put an 800 number on the zipper pull, offering a reward if found. That reassured me, and I decided to board the planned 7:30 flight.

As I boarded the flight, I saw that the bag was not on the planeside cart. I talked to the baggage handlers, who said that it might have been loaded already but they had no way of knowing. No frustration yet. Fortunately, the young Flemish man in the seat next to me was a pleasant co-traveler. Unfortunately, I had more important things to reflect upon: the pilot on the very small, propeller-driven plane looked younger than my son!

The plane arrived on time. I disembarked with the other passengers and walked over to the planeside baggage cart. No backpack of mine there. Well, there was the carousal possibility. The bags came up slowly, but soon enough they were all out. All except my backpack.

I did get a chance at that point to reflect on the source of frustration, concluding that frustration occurs when you have a problem but no resources (money, time, authority, help) to resolve it on your own. So, enlisting the help of others would be important.

Since Alaska Airlines does not fly into my local airport, there was nothing to be done except return to San Ignatio and call the Alaskan Airlines 800 number, hoping that I would find needed help. When I called, I was given the Alaskan Airlines baggage office number at the San Francisco airport. I called. No answer. I called again. No answer. I called a third time. No answer. I left three messages. No one called.

Giving up on that approach, I rang the 800 number again. As the woman on the other end, Zena, began to put me off, I told her she could not pass me off to an automated menu because that would frustrate me and I was not supposed to get frustrated, having given up frustration for Lent. She laughed sympathetically and called the San Francisco baggage office herself—with the same results I had obtained. She eventually reached a janitor, who put her online with a supervisor.

Eventually, I got my backpack back. When Mr. Wendell realized that my bag would not make the next flight out, that he had no idea to whom the bag really belonged, and that I did not have the claim number, he compared the Alaskan Air and United manifests and determined that I was the only female passenger transferring to any United flight at that time. Once he had my name, he entered the claim number with a red flag on my ticket information in the computer so that both Alaskan Airlines and United would have the claim number if needed. (I think Mr. Wendell would make a great FBI or CIA employee!) Zena then tracked the number. She found the bag on the 10:00 United flight, and I picked it up the next morning.

Thanks to Mr. Wendell and Zena, I was able to keep my Lenten pledge. A funny thing happens with Lenten pledges. When you get in the habit of doing or not doing things, Lent ends but the habit continues, a kind of *metanoia* in itself. Now I rarely experience frustration, which is good, for as that wise priest said, frustration does not come from God.

And Life Goes On

As an atheist, I accepted the challenge of raising special-needs children because the alternative, in my opinion, was unthinkable. After all, I told others, we do what we have to do; we take a bad hand and play it as well as we can. At least, that has been the way I had lived my life, without giving much conscious thought as to why.

My post-conversion acceptance was different. Not only did it have an element of forgiveness, but that forgiveness was also wrapped in loving awe, then, with the next *metanoia*, in deep gratitude, and now in a humbling sense of unworthiness.

The awe came when, after reading *Job*, I inventoried my life and saw how God had turned every challenge to good use. For every challenge, I could point out a positive outcome, for every bad thing a resultant good. As I tallied up all the good that has come from what looked like bad things, the next metanoic ripple carried me into a pool of gratitude for the knowledge (medicine, education, psychology, parenting) I would not have otherwise acquired, the knowledge–and more important, compassion, sibling love, and moral character–that my children developed, the ways in which I have been able to help others, the love my challenged children and grandchildren have brought out in others, and even the transference of many of my parenting experiences to the workplace that has had as much to do with my rise as a leader in my field as traditional training and education. For all the things I have listed and much more, I am eternally grateful.

As my gratitude has deepened, yet another metanoic ripple has carried me onward to a humbling sense of unworthiness, which is where I find myself swimming now: in a pond of trust, filled by God, wondering if I deserve to be here. God has entrusted me with some special challenges and has trusted me to meet those challenges. I want to be worthy of such trust, yet I fear I am not. I have done the best I could and have trusted God, in return, to take care of the rest. I still rely on simple trust as I wait for the next metanoic ripple.

As I was thinking all these things, I felt a nearly-imperceptible-but-clearly-loving, wispy touch. I have felt that touch before. When I feel that touch, I know I have gotten something right. Just what it is I have right, I am not one hundred percent certain, but I am pretty sure it has something to do with God wanting me to have these experiences out of love for me and wanting me to rely on Divine help with all challenges—the ones I have described, the ones I have not described, and the ones yet to come.

Silent Running

Just when I begin to think that I understand perhaps a small slice of God's grace, I find myself back at the beginning. Physical things happen to me that I do not understand. Mystical things happen to me that I do not understand. Where are these experiences supposed to lead me? Or, am I supposed to sit tight and let their transforming power alone affect me? I just don't know. So, confusion reigns.

While I am grateful to God for the unexpected and unexplainable healings, I have received, they, too, have left me in a state of confusion. Why would God intervene in my fate in this way? Am I supposed to be doing something in response?

When it comes to mystical experiences, I find myself even more confused. Are these personal, intimate gifts for maintaining in a private relationship or are they joy and knowledge to be shared with others? If the latter, then I do such a poor job that I have to think that any other person would be a better choice as recipient of such gifts. When I speak of such things, with rare exception, I meet with incredulity. So, again, I am back in the state of confusion.

Perhaps I should simply accept such grace—unearned and unconditional—as a gift of love from God, given to sinners and righteous alike because, in reality, there is nothing else I *can* do. Perhaps I should also accept my state of confusion as a gift and stop searching for clarity. Perhaps I should not worry whether people consider me sane. My state of confusion brings me closer to God. Should that not be enough? I try to value and love my state of confusion for it has been given to me by God.

More difficult to value and love are times when I am on silent running along this path that I do not see clearly and past rocks over which I stumble. Some of those times resemble dark nights, as described by St. John of the Cross (*Ascent of Mount Carmel*). Such things seemed buried in centuries-old mysticism—until I turned a bend in the path and walked out of the fields of sunshine into a deep, dark wood.

Dark Nights

I had taken no more than a few faltering steps with God before I learned about the dark nights of the senses and spirit. First, Jean experienced this phenomenon. Then I experienced it. In that Divinely inimitable way that I have grown to appreciate, God prepared me for my experience by allowing me to participate in Jean's.

Jean's Dark Night

One evening, as I was working late, Jean burst into my office, eyes large and frightened. "Beth," she exclaimed. "I think the Evil One is after me!"

I had never heard Jean or anyone else speak in those terms before, so I was taken aback. "What do you mean?" I asked.

"I suddenly feel estranged from God," she replied.

Jean came by nearly every evening after that, and we prayed. Always for the same thing: to bring Jean back to where she had been spiritually, not realizing that going through the dark night was necessary if Jean were to meet a new dawn and develop a closer relationship with God. As soon as her faith reared its head, it was stomped into the dust again. I began praying for her every day for hours.

Weeks later, having indeed emerged into daylight, Jean told me that 18 years earlier she had met someone she thought was her guardian angel. He had said to her, "One day you may experience spiritual trial. Should that ever happen to you, I hope that you will have someone at your side to help you."

She did. Ironically, Jean, who had served as God's instrument to shepherd me back to the flock, had me at her side. Even though I did not know what to do, I had God to guide me. So, Jean, though unaware of it, had God at her side throughout her ordeal. I was clearly only a conduit, through which God guided Jean through the dark night and deposited her once again in the light.

Similarly, Jean had been simply a conduit for God to convert me. Through observations, I came to know that Jean is no paragon of perfection as I originally thought. I caught her in a number of lies about minor things in which the truth would have served her better. She often walked by the law, thinking that if she followed all the rules, she would "earn salvation" and "make up for her sin" rather than by the spirit, growing closer to God through repentance, confession, and contemplation. At one point, I wondered why God would use her to reach me—until I realized how often God uses imperfection, including me, for divine purposes. Upon reflection, it seems perfectly natural that God would use Jean. After all, she was going to need me for her dark night. Moreover, it seems arrogant to assume that I deserved an angel or a saint. Praise God for Divine use of imperfect people! Otherwise, I would not have had the opportunity to help Jean or anyone else—and had I not shared Jean's dark night, mine would have been frightening, rather than illuminating.

My Dark Night

To understand my difficulties with silent running, one needs to realize that God spoils me. That is not only my perception; that is the perception of many who know me. I do not have to wait for answers to prayers—sometimes they come before I even ask or in lieu of my asking. Nearly any time I have tried to help someone else, divine intervention and the people who come with it carry the action forward faster and better than I ever could alone.

So, for more than four years after my conversion, I tripped merrily along, secure in the presence of God. Even if I were sleeping, I knew God would keep away nightmares, and I had none. Throughout the day, at work or home, I could feel the presence of God. God's presence had become the core of my life.

Then the *wham!* day came—and the next day and the next and so on for more than three weeks. I had no sense of God's presence for day after day. It would have been easy to think that all my previous experience with the Presence of God had been imagined. That's the way our human minds work. The past is gone; the present is where we live; the future we look forward to if we don't like the present. I realized during the early days of this experience that I had a choice. I could choose to believe in spite of the absence of any spiritual connectiveness. I guess that is what faith is: choosing to believe.

What kept me going was knowing that Mother Theresa had gone through a dark night for *years*. Why? That is a question that only God can answer, but Thomas à Kempis in *The Imitation of Christ* suggests a way of viewing the experience—a more humble one than my initial response of wailing and begging for the lifting of the dark night—that I find helpful:

> *Do you think that you will always have spiritual consolations as you desire? My saints did not always have them. Instead, they had many afflictions, temptations of various kinds, and great desolation. Yet they bore them all patiently. They placed their confidence in God rather than in themselves, knowing that the sufferings of this life are not worthy to be compared with the glory that is to come. And you—do you wish to have at once that which others have scarcely obtained after many tears and great labors? Wait for the Lord, act bravely, and have courage. Do not lose trust.*

I began to understand much better what St. John of the Cross meant when he said that the dark night is a positive thing, an opportunity to grow spiritually, a cleansing and purification. It is yet another *metanoia*. Barbara Yoder, in discussing the dark night of the soul in *The Overcomer's Annointing*, asks, "Could it be that God is beginning to get your attention in a way that He has not had it before?" After all, God transformed the darkness at the very beginning of time and throughout history and even until today continues to transform darkness. Is *metanoia* anything more than the transformation of our internal darkness into something else? Can we be transformed at all if we avoid the darkness?

Likewise, Thomas Merton in *Contemplative Prayer* describes the dark night as a time that "marks the transfer of the full, free control of our inner life into the hands of a superior power." I suppose my fear and frustration came from no longer being able to *feel* that superior power after months of habituation.

Recently I heard a homily in which the priest talked about the Word, as in that which was in the beginning, is now, and always will be. "Wherever there is darkness," the priest said, "the Word is there to bring light. We may not see the Light, but the Light is there." I guess it is like when the sun goes down but is still there.

I did not want to go into that dark night because, like people in a bygone era frightened by solar eclipses, I worried that the sun might never return. I was afraid of what I would lose. I did not understand one iota of what powerful transformation I would gain by trusting my inner life to the unfelt Divine.

Now that the Presence is palpably back in my life, I don't think I will ever again take it for granted. More than that, though, I know that I do have faith. If it seems weak, I can choose to believe and to ask God to increase my faith. God will do it.

As much as I did not want to go through a dark night myself, I am now grateful that God gifted me with this experience. Now, too, I will not fear another dark night should God want to so gift me again. I will know that even if I cannot feel God's presence, God is with me always. I know that I *can* believe by volition. Simply choosing to believe must be even more gratifying to God than believing because the jaws of the "Hound of Heaven" have rested around one's ankle. At the same time, I no longer fear transformation. I welcome it.

Trust

Living in a silent running mode is all about trust. There can be no real faith without trust. Trust, though, can be elusive and difficult to maintain, as much as we may protest that we *do* trust.

"Pray, hope and don't worry," St. Pio once said. "Worry is useless. God is merciful and will hear your prayers. Prayer is the best weapon we have. It is the key to God's heart."

If we hand a problem over to God and then worry about it, is that trust? By worrying about it, we have taken the problem back. I have had two vivid reminders that a problem handed over is a problem resolved, regardless of how things may seem.

The Foolishness of Taking Things Back

Usually, after asking God for help, I go on to other things, finding that God has a way of taking care of things better than we can imagine. Sometimes, though. I have been foolish enough not to put all worry aside after prayer, resulting in an unnecessary waste of energy and emotion!

A couple of years ago, for example, I had made a mistake that could have extremely serious repercussions by signing a document without reading it thoroughly. By doing so, I had committed my organization to pay thousands of dollars for a contract I had no authorization to make, yet the work had already been done. Media attention was threatened on Friday by the party not getting paid for that work. I left the office not knowing what the situation would be on Monday, but the next-higher office was clearly frightened by the whole situation. And then the day ended.

Needless to say, I fretted all weekend. Of course, I asked God for help right in the beginning, and then I embarked on a fretting spree. On Sunday, as I fretted when

I should have been praying, I suddenly saw the image of a tug-of-war, and I immediately understood that the rope symbolized my work problem. At the same time, I heard the words very clearly, "Let Me have it!"

Startled, I immediately dropped my end of the rope, which went slack, and then the image disappeared. My worry had disappeared, too. No more fretting. I could pay attention to prayer.

Truly, I had left the problem behind. In fact, I completely forgot about it and went on peacefully with the rest of Sunday since now God really did have the problem. On Monday, I went to work, still in a peaceful mood.

I had nearly completely forgotten about the whole issue when I got a call from a specialist who said he had been asked to come in early and work on "my" problem. In so doing, he found that what had happened to me represented a serious glitch in the system that could cause all kinds of unauthorized spending. It was being fixed, and the party expecting payment was actually going to get paid, along with several other parties who were discovered to have performed services for other divisions and not been paid! Not only that, I was being lauded because my mistake uncovered a serious problem with the system.

I was a hero! More important, I had another example of God knowing best, of God turning bad into good, and of the fact that we can, and should, trust God with anything and everything *and not fret*! As they say, just "let go, and let God..."

The lesson I learned that weekend is one that Max Lucado explicates in *When God Whispers Your Name*. When we don't know what to do we should just sit tight until God does God's thing, i.e. we should get out of God's way. I was told to "let Me have it" because I was in God's way. In cases like this, according to Lucado, "our job is to pray and wait. Nothing more is necessary."

Ruthless Trust

That experience, you would think, should have taught me always to trust God. Yet, I once again had some moments of fretting only a year later.

I was on a business trip in Maryland. With me was a colleague who had moved to the US from the Middle East, and quite coincidentally another colleague living in the Middle East had come to the US on a business trip. Both were Muslim; both were devout. We met several times for dinner, and at one point, we decided to do some shopping, mainly to help our visiting colleague buy souvenirs for his family. At a Sears store, where our colleague wanted to check out luggage, I, too, decided to make a small purchase. Somewhat later, after the rounds of several stores, I decided to make another small purchase. I pulled out my credit cards. My bank card was missing! I figured I had probably dropped it at the Sears store when I pulled out my Sears card. Just in case, though, my two colleagues and I retraced all our steps throughout the mall, carefully inspecting the floor for any sign of my card. No sign.

Then, we talked to the clerk who had waited on us at the Sears store. No, she had not seen any of my credit cards drop, and no one had turned my card in.

Now I was seriously concerned. My colleagues thought that the card was probably in my hotel room, but I could not imagine where. Canceling the card if I really had it would complicate my trip since I would then be without access to my bank account. Of course, if it were lost, I needed to cancel it to prevent unauthorized use. I called my bank and was told to check my room first, then let them know. There was a 6:00 deadline, after which the card could not be canceled until the following day.

It was already 4:30, and my colleagues were dallying. "Just one more store," one of them said. "We're not going to get another chance to shop. Don't worry. The card will be in your room. Allah always takes care of you."

It was after 6:00 when we finally reached the hotel. We went to my room and looked around, but we found nothing. It being too late to call the bank that day, I opened a bottle of something to drink—I don't recall what it was now—and poured out drinks for all three of us.

While I was doing that, one of my colleagues sat down at my desk. Seeing a book there, he opened it to see what I was reading.

"You have time to read while here?" he asked.

"Oh, I was reading it on the plane. I have not had a minute here to read anything."

He flipped through the book, and out fell my bank card. I forgot that I had used it to buy food on the plane and, not being able to reach my purse, had placed the card in the book as a bookmark, planning to put it in my purse later but then forgetting.

"I told you Allah always takes care of you," my colleague said, handing me the card. "You should trust Allah, you know." He laughed and handed me the book: *Ruthless Trust: The Ragamuffin's Path to God* (Brendan Manning).

I have subsequently wondered whether this was coincidence or a divine lesson on trust. No matter how great our faith, we all need that lesson occasionally. The wonderful thing is that when we lack trust in God, we can always ask God to help us trust more. I believe that God delights in answering such prayers.

When God Comes

God comes to me most frequently in the humble moments of my life. In the early morning and late evening when I take some moments for contemplation. In the early evening, when I take a walk around my beloved San Ignatio or on Old Mission grounds. Sometimes when I am driving, often when I am thinking about God but just as often when I am not, when I am simply trying to drive within the lines, a skill that does not come naturally to someone who learned first to drive a tractor in the wide open farm fields.

God comes to me at meetings when I let my mind focus on God's presence. I have been blessed with the ability to multi-task although once when I was called upon by my boss's boss to explain something at a high-level meeting, I had to admit to not being present in the boss's moment. I probably could have admitted that I was present, instead, in the Boss's (God's) moment because that individual had strong faith. However, being a coward in the midst of such an august secular group, I simply said that I had been "distant" for a moment. My generally irritable boss's boss could have become angry, but instead he laughed and said, "clearly, very distant."

At the proud moments, though, I find God missing. Actually, I don't find God at all in them because I am not looking for God. I am looking at myself. Those are empty moments. The fulfilling ones are where I look for—and find—God with me.

God comes, too, to the humble places in my life. I meet God in the open fields, on the mountaintops, and on the mission grounds.

The Old Mission in San Ignatio is one of those humble places. Built by Indians with uneven floor tiles preserving paw prints of animals that ran across the tiles as they were baking in the sun, the Old Mission promotes a deep awareness of God's presence that is especially strong in early mornings at the end of December when light from the rising sun enters an upper window, bounces against the statues behind the altar, and then splays all the way down the middle aisle.

People ask me why I would live in a poor, small, farming area in a narrow valley with a town center that is more Mexican than American when I hold a high-powered position, involving much international work and travel. I tell them that the fields are why. The mountains are why. The simplicity is why. The humility of the population is why. God is why.

Likewise, ten years ago I walked up a hill on the outskirts of Tbilisi, Georgia in an impoverished, Muslim neighborhood. Two other members of the international consulting team formed to help the Ministry of Education develop national exams accompanied me on the trek of religious buildings in the city. We first visited an Orthodox Cathedral, where the new archbishop happened to be in the process of being welcomed when we entered. Then, about a half-mile away, we walked up to a synagogue that, not knowing what to do with foreign women, let the Russian team member (a woman) and me sit where synagogues do not usually allow women so that we could be with our Jewish team member (a man) from Holland. Finally, as the day was nearing its end, we trudged up the hill, at the top of which stood the simple mosque. We were surprised that the door was open. Soon after we entered, the imam showed up. Before him stood a Russian Orthodox believer from Moscow, a Jew from Amsterdam, and an atheist from the United States. The Russian and I covering our hair appropriately, we entered a small room with old, worn rugs on the floor. An ancient page from the Qu'ran was encased in a stand along one wall. The imam patiently and proudly pointed out religiously important aspects of the mosque. Standing there, I felt something special, special enough that I wanted to linger. I did not recognize it at the time. Now I know that I was sensing the presence of God.

Sacraments

The sacraments kept me going when in silent running. I believe that we have been given the sacraments for many reasons, but one very good reason is to guide us through the dark moments in our lives and bring us back out into the light. Even when we feel no Presence at all, the sacraments force us to pray. Perhaps the prayer feels dry or empty, but it is prayer nonetheless. As with any prayer, dry or electrified by God's presence, there is a maker of the prayer and a receiver of the prayer. Whether or not God's presence is felt, God remains an integral part of the praying. Even if the action does not take the shape of an interaction, God is present always.

Confession

Recently, a retreat I had been attending included the opportunity for confession. There were four priests, one of whom had been ordained 45 days earlier. It was into the hands of this latter priest that I fell.

The confession I brought to him was weighty, involved circumstances well beyond my control, and had serious implications for the future, including my own physical safety. This, I thought, would be a challenge for a new priest, and, as I spoke, I could see in his eyes a reflection of the overwhelming nature of what I was bringing to him. I began to feel sorry for bringing it when suddenly his demeanor changed. So did mine. We were not alone.

We were so not alone that I felt like I was talking with God Himself. If I had had any lingering doubt about God being present through the priest in the sacrament of confession, this experience would have extirpated any root of disbelief.

The priest did not give me a penance. He gave me a task. Now, that's exactly what God would do! The task pulled me back onto the path I needed to be on. I guess deep down, no matter how I try to become a Mary, I remain a Martha. The priest did not know that, but God did.

Eucharist

Of all the sacraments, the Eucharist is my favorite. It is in the Eucharist we know, no matter what else may be going on in our lives at the time, that God is present. God must be present, or there is no Eucharist. Of all the parts of the Eucharist, my favorite is the silent time for prayer after receiving the host. With God within and God without, the universe is complete, and I find it easy to rest in contemplation of the perfection of it all (if in the silent running mode) and in the ambient love (if in the Presence mode). Either way the Eucharist opens the door to transformation and ever-continuing conversion.

Years before I converted to Catholicism, I studied Greek. I remember only a few words, mostly medical terms or greetings, from those days, but one very common word I do recall: *efkharisto*, meaning *thank you*. The root of that word is also the root of *efkharist, eucharist*. It would seem appropriate, then, to leave each Eucharist with one last word to God: *efkharisto*. I like to do that!

The End, for Now

With this attention to how important the sacraments have become in my life, I close this book of my walk with God so far. There are times that I wish I could go through this life again, even with all of its trials, but this time secure in my knowledge of the love of God and with an attitude of gratitude and humility—to remove the imperfections with which I have greeted this life. Then I realize that we have not been given this life in order to enjoy being perfect but have inherited a sinful condition and been given an opportunity in this life to learn, to experience God's grace, and to become "perfect, even as [our] Father is perfect" (*Matthew* 5:48).

The final chapter of this book ends as the first chapter began—with prayer. I know that whatever the first chapter of the next book in my life will bring, it will begin with prayer. My life these days is becoming an unending prayer. This life prayer is not characterized by memorized verses and long recitations of praise and pleas although those did help in the dark period. Rather, my life prayer is characterized by fluid movement within a limbic, pre-cognitive state, alternating between profane action and sacred stillness. I find myself drawn to places where I can be alone even though I am an extrovert by nature. I have not turned on a television set in the many hotel rooms I have occupied over the past three years during my constant travels because I crave the silence where I find God.

That is not to say that the profane does not inappropriately intrude into the sacred or that I don't occasionally march off in quite the opposite direction from the one in which God would have me go. Nor does it mean that I never question my sanity or want to check to see if my sensory array has gone awry when it comes to manifestations. At the same time, I do not forget about Occam's razor (*lex parsimoniae)*, a heuristic originating from Newton in which one admits no more natural causes than necessary for a hypothesis, spawning the related notion that the simplest explanation, however implausible, is likely the truth. Things such as I have experienced do happen, and yet there are times I don't want to accept that they do, times that I try to run from them. These are indeed moments that make me feel the need for repentant confession either through the intercession of a priest or, if one is not available, directly to God in prayer that remains fixed at the deepest levels of unconscious expression without bubbling to the surface as a formed linguistic utterance.

What is that prayer? Well, if it were somehow to break through to the surface and take the form of conscious words, it would go something like the following:

"Lord, please keep Your promise to be with me always. Teach me. I have much to learn. Know that I want to do whatever You ask of me. If I stray in doing Your will, it is from human weakness, and I fully regret each step gone awry. I implicitly trust You in everything but especially to develop in me the strength and humility I require to carry out Your every task. I sense within every fiber of my being that You will help me with nary a plea, but, my being human, You and I both know that I am going to streak to You for help at times. When all is said and done, in this life, I need only Your love and guidance. Thank you for everything you have given to me, taken from me, or made me work through. Thank you for every moment of glory and even more for every moment of humiliation. Most especially thank You for loving me and letting me love You, for letting me be part of Your love story."

I know now why Jesus, St. Francis, and many others spent so much time in the wilderness—deserts, mountains, or caves—being alone with God. They were listening, receiving, growing, uniting, loving, and being loved. They were being still and encountering God.

CPSIA information can be obtained at www.ICGtesting.com
Printed in the USA
BVOW050356101011

273166BV00006B/2/P